Positive
Action

People Making the World a Better Place

Greg Goodmacher

JN116649

NATIONAL
GEOGRAPHIC
LEARNING

Australia · Brazil · Mexico · Singapore · United Kingdom · United States

Positive Action—People Making the World a Better Place

Greg Goodmacher

© 2023 Cengage Learning K.K.

Photo credits appear on page 122, which constitutes a continuation of the copyright page.

ISBN: 978-4-86312-396-0

National Geographic Learning | Cengage Learning K.K.
No. 2 Funato Building 5th Floor
1-11-11 Kudankita, Chiyoda-ku
Tokyo 102-0073
Japan

Tel: 03-3511-4392
Fax: 03-3511-4391

Positive Action aims to increase your confidence in using English and teach you ways to be a more active member of your community. It is a multifaceted language-learning textbook with inspirational stories encouraging students like you to help others.

If you often pay attention to local and global news, you might already know about issues such as women's rights, climate change, food waste, and bullying. Maybe you have already studied these and other social problems. Now, you get a chance to read, listen, talk, write, and think about these in English.

I hope you will take on a challenge that goes beyond only thinking about problems. The challenge is for you and your classmates to help reduce the severity of social and global problems. It is easy to get depressed by these problems and feel that solutions do not exist or that students are powerless.

This textbook tells the stories of female and male children, teenagers, and adults around the world who positively act to help others. These individuals have cleaned communities, saved wildlife, encouraged sick people, and become role models. Person to person, day by day, they work to make the world a better place.

As you study these active world citizens, your English communication skills will also improve. In addition, developing competency in the reading, vocabulary, critical thinking, and oral communication strategies you will come across in this textbook will aid you in scoring higher points on English proficiency tests.

After finishing this textbook, you will probably realize that you have gained the ability to communicate effectively and make the world a better place. Ordinary people like you are turning the world into a more positive place to live.

I believe you will feel proud of yourself and your friends after completing some of the suggested actions in this textbook and using English to share your experiences and opinions.

Greg Goodmacher

Table of Contents

To the Student   3
To the Teacher   6
How to Access the Audio Online   9

Unit	Title	Featured Person(s)	
1	**Resourcefulness**	**William Kamkwamba** [Malawi, Africa]	▶
2	**Women's Rights**	**Malala Yousafzai** [Pakistan]	▶
3	**Emotional Support**	**Parker Todd** [the US]	▶
4	**Poaching**	**Female Anti-poaching Rangers** [South Africa]	▶
5	**Reforestation**	**Jadav Payeng** [India]	▶
6	**Bullying**	**Emily-Anne Rigal** [the US]	▶
7	**Food Waste**	**Rayner Loi** [Singapore]	▶
8	**Climate Change**	**Greta Thunberg** [Sweden]	▶
9	**Hair Donation**	**Supporters of Bald Children** [around the world]	▶
10	**Homeless People**	**Joshua Coombes** [the UK]	▶
11	**Cleaner Places**	**Nadia Sparkes** [the UK]	▶
12	**Artworks**	**Chris Jordan** [the US]	▶
13	**Suicide Prevention**	**Kevin Hines** [the US]	▶
14	**Peacebuilding**	**Leymah Gbowee** [Liberia, Africa]	▶

Introduction to the Passage	Action to Take	Page
An undereducated boy studies by himself in order to save starving people in his community.	**Help people in Africa**	10
A girl shot by a Taliban soldier keeps fighting for peace and promotes educational projects.	**Present on a female worker**	18
A boy fighting a disease creates a comic book in order to encourage other sick children.	**Volunteer for patients**	26
The world's first group of all-female rangers starts protecting wildlife from armed poachers.	**Protect endangered animal species**	34
A young man shocked by the death of animals and plants in his village starts growing a forest.	**Plant trees**	42
A bullied girl turns into a bully, but finally becomes an anti-bullying activist.	**Create a kindness calendar**	50
A student who learned about food insecurity invents an AI system to reduce food waste.	**Reduce food waste at home**	58
A world famous activist's first protest was sitting alone with a sign as a climate strike.	**Make efforts to be eco-friendly**	66
Many people try to help hairless children suffering from several kinds of difficulties.	**Present about donating body parts**	74
A hairdresser offers his skills to the homeless and starts "DoSomethingForNothing."	**Help the homeless**	82
A campaign started by a girl called Trash Girl leads to worldwide clean-up activities.	**Organize a cleaning event**	90
Art has the power to bring people's attention to social and global problems.	**Create art about a global issue**	98
A survivor of a suicide attempt decides to help others by talking about his mental struggles.	**Create a poster to prevent suicide**	106
A victim of violence overcomes wartime hardships and becomes a peacebuilder.	**Present on a peacebuilder**	114

To the Teacher

Positive Action is aimed at intermediate-level students and helps them develop reading, listening, speaking, and critical thinking skills. There are 14 units in this textbook, and each unit has eight pages. A variety of exercises in each unit stimulate students and reinforce content knowledge and vocabulary retention.

The following activities progress step by step to assist students in developing English skills. In addition, the textbook offers suggestions for in- and out-of-class activities. Through these activities and the reading passages, students can realize they have the power and abilities to effect positive change in their communities.

Getting Ready

This section contains four photographs and simple questions that stimulate students to think about their lives and significant social and global issues. As a result, students become ready for the unit's contents.

Vocabulary

Students learn seven key vocabulary items chosen from the reading passage through two different exercises.

A Seven sentences have one targeted vocabulary item printed in bold font. Students practice guessing the meanings of these words from the context of surrounding words. These essential words are recycled throughout the unit and often appear in later units.

B Students continue reading and vocabulary development by examining sentences with one missing word and choosing which of the targeted vocabulary items from Exercise A they should write in the blanks.

(((◉))) $\frac{A}{00}$ Where a CD icon is placed, the audio for this exercise is only available on the audio CDs.

Reading

The reading passages, approximately 600 words each, tell the inspirational stories of boys, girls, men, and women from various regions of the world. These individuals provide examples of people taking positive action to reduce various social and global problems and help others. Their stories will inspire students to do good and introduce them to significant issues. Exercises A, B, and C follow the passages.

A   This short activity requires students to consider the passage's overall meaning. Students read four choices and choose the best one that could serve as the passage's title. Through this exercise, students work on the ability to summarize the central meaning of a passage.

B   This exercise has students examine a list of reported events in the story. Then, students must decide on the correct order. An activity like this requires students to review and comprehend the reading and demonstrate they understand the flow of events.

C   This is a unique variation of the typical true or false reading comprehension activity that many textbooks include. This particular exercise makes students demonstrate their textual comprehension. Students must skim the material to decide on the correctness of sentences. If students determine that the information in the sentence is incorrect, they rewrite the false statement as a correct one.

Listening

Students work on two different types of listening activities that are connected with the reading section.

A   You might not find the same activity in other textbooks. This unusual activity develops the ability to scan for information while listening to questions. First, students listen to questions about the story that they have read. Then, they must scan the reading passage and choose which of the four choices is the best response to each question. Depending on their level, students might or might not correctly comprehend the questions and find the answers. Replay the questions as often as needed. You could also allow students to discuss the questions and their answers.

B   This cloze listening activity introduces even more inspirational stories of people taking positive action to help others. In most cases, the person or people students learn about reside in a different part of the world than those people the reading passages concentrate on.

Your Own Ideas

In this section, students can verbally express their ideas regarding questions that touch on the topic or topics in the reading passages. The textbook prepares students to express their opinions.

A Students read the questions and model answers. Then, they choose the most appropriate responses to the questions.

(CD icon) $\frac{A}{00}$ Where a CD icon is placed, the audio for this exercise is only available on the audio CDs.

B Using the questions in Exercise A, students communicate their original opinions and experiences to partners.

Critical Thinking

Critically analyzing statements and expressing opinions in a foreign language can be difficult. This section makes it easier.

A Since everyone benefits from specific examples, students read examples of ways to express responses that range from "strongly agree" to "strongly disagree." After reading the examples, students examine three statements that thematically connect with the particular unit they are studying. Then, students must deeply consider the meanings of those statements and decide the degree to which they agree or disagree. After coming to a conclusion, students write the reasons for their responses.

B Students share and discuss their conclusions about the three statements in Exercise A with others.

Taking Action

Every person on Earth should consider a problem and then take positive action toward a solution. Therefore, each unit concludes with a project-type activity where students are asked to take action by following three steps to make the world better.

Acknowledgments The author would like to thank Professor Kip Cates, Professor David Peaty, and the Global Issues in Language (GILE) Special Interest Section of JALT for inspiring me to develop teaching materials for GILE content-based EFL classes.

How to Access the Audio Online

For activities with a headset icon ($\frac{A}{00}$), the audio is available at the website below.

https://ngljapan.com/posiactn-audio/

You can access the audio as outlined below.

❶ Visit the website above.

❷ Click the link to the content you would like to listen to.

Alternatively, scan the QR code with a smartphone or tablet to visit the website above.

....

NOTICE

For activities with a CD icon ($\frac{A}{00}$), the audio is only available on the audio CDs the teacher has.

Unit 1

Resourcefulness

William Kamkwamba

Getting Ready

▶ Work in pairs. Look at the pictures and discuss the questions below.

1. What is the name of this continent? What do you know about it?

2. What is the name of this object? What can it be used for?

3. Where are these people? How often do you go to a place like this?

4. Do you like to speak in front of many people? Why or why not?

Vocabulary

A Read the sentences and guess the meanings of the bold words.

1. I did not finish high school or go to college. Some people think I am **undereducated**.

2. His brothers laughed at him when he first played guitar, but he did not **give up** playing it. Today, he is a famous musician.

3. My brother lost the use of his eyes. A specially trained dog helped him to **overcome** both his sadness and physical challenges.

4. **Impoverished** people are struggling to live. They do not have safe homes and enough food, money, and health care.

5. A long period of hot weather without rain causes a **drought**.

6. The terrible weather conditions that killed most of the plants and the animals resulted in a **famine**. Millions of people died because they could not find food.

7. Students **drop out** of school for different reasons. Some are not interested in studying, and some lack money to pay for school.

B Fill in the blanks with the bold words above. Change the form if necessary. A 58

Ex. Some newspapers report that North Korea has many _impoverished_ people.

---

1. By working after school and on weekends to save money, she did not have to _____ her dream of studying abroad.

2. During the _____, people ate insects, grass, and leaves.

3. Because of the _____, we could not grow rice.

4. She decided to _____ of college and start a technology company.

5. Usually, _____ people receive lower salaries than college graduates.

6. I had to _____ many language and cultural problems after I moved to another country.

Reading

▶ Read the passage. Then, answer the following questions.

William at the African Leadership Academy in Johannesburg, South Africa

In the 1990s, millions of people worldwide listened to the words of a poor, **undereducated** African teenager named William Kamkwamba. He simply said, "Whatever happens, don't **give up**." People paid attention to William because he had **overcome** problems that would make most of us lose hope.

He was born on August 5, 1987, in Malawi, Africa, one of the most **impoverished** countries in the world. Many Malawians lacked electricity in their homes, money for education, and food to stay healthy.

The year that William turned 14, very little rain fell. The **drought** dried up the ground. Food was almost impossible to buy or find. Even farming families like William's suffered from **famine**. His family ate one small meal of corn flour and water a day. Around his village, thousands of people were begging for food and dying. Everyone in his family nearly died.

He also had to **drop out** of school. His father could not pay the school tuition. However, William loved learning and studying. He borrowed books, especially science books, from a library. Many of them were English-language books, but he could barely read English. Teaching himself, William carefully studied the pictures and guessed the meanings of English words.

One day, he borrowed an American junior high school textbook titled *Using Energy*. The book changed his life. For the first time, he learned about windmills.

The book inspired him. He dreamed of building windmills to provide electricity to his home and pump water from the ground to the family farm. In addition, he wanted everyone in his community to have food. Without training and proper tools, he started building a windmill using parts from an old bicycle, broken machines, and pieces of wood. His neighbors thought he was a crazy boy. However, the windmill he built in his home's front yard worked. For the first time, his family's home had lights. Only two percent of Malawians had electricity in their homes then.

1
2
3
4
5
6
7
8
9
10
11
12
13
14
15
16
17
18
19
20
21
22
23
24
25
26
27
28
29
30
31
32

William later built a second windmill to bring water to his home and farm. His irrigation windmill helped his family and village to grow more vegetables. Everyone had more food. Before this windmill, people had to carry water by hand, and they could only raise vegetables when lots of rain fell.

The unschooled boy who built a windmill became a topic of conversation in Malawi. First, newspapers wrote about William and his creation. Then, he was invited to talk at an international conference in a big city far from his home.

Although William was shy and his English was very basic, he explained to an audience of highly educated people how he built a windmill from pieces of garbage. He also shared plans to help his community with more windmills. International media videotaped his speech.

Millions of people around the world heard his story. They were impressed. Many people collected money to help him return to school. While studying, he taught science to other students and built more windmills.

A journalist helped him to write a book about his life. The book became internationally famous. After that, a movie company made a film about William.

With the assistance of fans worldwide and the money from book sales, he went to the US, where he graduated from college. Today, William uses his fame, education, and money to help other poor Africans go to school and to develop successful businesses across Africa. He still advises, "Whatever happens, don't give up."

William's cousin is climbing a windmill providing power to the Kamkwamba family farm.

13

A What would be the best title for the passage?

    a. Building Windmills in Africa

    b. Good Books about Energy

    c. The Benefits of Windmills

    d. A Boy Who Would Not Give Up

B Write numbers to show the order of the events.

    __1__   William was born in Malawi.

    _____   He decided to make his first windmill.

    _____   There was a drought that caused the deaths of many people.

    _____   He learned about windmills.

    _____   People around the world helped him return to school.

    _____   He built other windmills and taught science.

    __7__   Now, he uses his fame, education, and money to help others.

C Circle "C" for the correct information and "I" for the incorrect information. If the information is incorrect, revise the sentence.

    Ex. Malawi is one of the richest countries in the world.

        [C /(I)]   *Malawi is one of the most impoverished countries in the world.*

    1. Many Malawians could not use lights and computers at home.

        [C / I] _____

    2. Many people died after a terrible flood in Malawi in 1987.

        [C / I] _____

    3. William made a windmill using garbage.

        [C / I] _____

    4. William's English was excellent when he spoke at the first conference in his life.

        [C / I] _____

5. Many people around the world helped William to pay for school.

[C / I] _____

6. William decided to help other Africans after graduating from college.

[C / I] _____

Listening

A Listen to the questions while scanning the passage and circle the best answers.

A
04-07

1. **a.** corn flour **b.** wheat flour **c.** rice flour **d.** sunflowers

2. **a.** elementary school **b.** junior high school **c.** high school **d.** college

3. **a.** billions **b.** millions **c.** thousands **d.** hundreds

4. **a.** scientist **b.** teacher **c.** journalist **d.** engineer

B Listen to the story and complete the script below.

A
08

Famous Scholars

William reminds me of two famous _____. The first is Abraham Lincoln, who _____ the 16th president of the United _____. According to stories, Abraham Lincoln studied _____ himself to become a lawyer.

The _____ person is Fukuzawa Yukichi. Although he was _____ into a family of low-ranking samurai, he studied _____. Despite many _____, he learned several languages _____ became one of Japan's greatest _____.

Abraham Lincoln

Fukuzawa Yukichi

Your Own Ideas

A Match the questions with the answers.

1. How do you rate yourself as a student? Why do you think so? _____

2. What do you want to learn at school and outside of school? _____

3. What adjectives would you use to describe William and yourself? _____

4. Can you tell us about a time when you struggled to succeed at a difficult task? _____

5. What are three inventions that you are grateful for? Why? _____

6. What valuable lessons or information have you learned from books? _____

a. At school, I'd like to learn to express my opinion in English. Outside of school, I want to learn how to drive a car.

b. I think that I'm a good student. My test scores are usually high, and I almost always do my homework.

c. I have learned how to create a blog. I have also learned a lot about world history.

d. William is caring and intelligent. I'm shy and a little lazy.

e. I'm grateful for my smartphone, video games, and the internet. With these, I can both play games and learn about the world.

f. The most difficult struggle for me was quickly learning the duties of my part-time job.

B Work in pairs. Take turns asking the questions above and answering with your own ideas.

Critical Thinking

A Read each statement below and write your opinion using one of the five key phrases in the example.

Ex. Libraries should lend books, magazines, and building tools to people in their neighborhoods.

- **I strongly agree.** Tools are useful. Poor people could make furniture, gifts, and repair homes.
- **I somewhat agree.** People can improve their lives with tools, but some tools are dangerous.
- **I'm not sure.** I've never thought about this topic since I seldom use libraries.
- **I somewhat disagree.** Our tax money would pay for tools, and perhaps few people would use them.
- **I strongly disagree.** People should buy their own books, magazines, and tools.

---

1. Our government should spend money helping people in other countries.

   _____

2. Japan needs to use more renewable forms of energy.

   _____

3. Education from elementary school to college should be free for everyone.

   _____

B Share your opinions with your classmates.

Taking Action

▶ Follow the steps to take action.

Step 1 Research three NPOs that help people in Africa. Then, choose the one you believe does the most valuable work and write a short summary about it.

Step 2 In a small group, read your summaries and choose the NPO you want to help.

Step 3 Think of an action you can take to help the organization. For example, you might collect money or goods and donate those.

Women's Rights

Malala Yousafzai

Getting Ready

▶ Work in pairs. Look at the pictures and discuss the questions below.

1. In many countries, fewer girls go to school than boys. Why is that?

2. Are boys and girls treated equally at schools in your country?

3. Do men and women with the same jobs get paid equally in most workplaces?

4. Why are most countries and companies led by men?

Vocabulary

A Read the sentences and guess the meanings of the bold words.

1. The policeman tried to stop the drunk man, but he reacted **violently**. He hit the policeman.

2. **Despite** lacking a college education, she became a company president.

3. War is scary. Most soldiers feel **fear** when the enemy is shooting at them.

4. Both Steven Jobs, the first leader of Apple, and Mark Zuckerberg, Facebook's leader, **founded** their companies in their early 20s.

5. I am so **passionate** about protecting nature that I spend almost all my time and money helping save plants and animals.

6. The robber showed a gun to the bank clerk and **threatened** to shoot the clerk if he refused to give the money to the robber.

7. Bob is an animal-rights **advocate**. He believes that zoos are cruel, and he is against medical experiments with animals.

B Fill in the blanks with the bold words above. Change the form if necessary.

> **Ex.** The angry children tried to solve the problem _violently_, so the teacher had to stop their fight.

1. The people who _____ the United States of America were all men.

2. I am _____ about human rights. I strongly believe that all humans are equal, so I participate in demonstrations for equal rights.

3. His body shook with _____ for a long time after the fighting ended.

4. To tell others that you will hurt them is to _____ those people.

5. _____ working harder than all the men, she never became manager.

6. Women can vote today thanks to the _____ who fought for women's rights.

Reading

▶ Read the passage. Then, answer the following questions.

Eleven-year-old Malala at home in Mingora, Pakistan, on March 26, 2009

Malala Yousafzai was born in Mingora, a small village in an impoverished region of Pakistan. The people of Mingora traditionally allowed females and males to study. Then, the Taliban, who **violently** opposed women's rights, came to Mingora when she was a girl. **Despite** her **fear**, she publicly spoke up about a girl's right to an education. Then, a Taliban soldier shot her on her way home from school.

Ziauddin, her father, encouraged her to study and fulfill her dream of becoming a doctor. As a child, Malala enthusiastically studied English, two local languages, and other subjects at a school her father **founded**. **Passionate** about learning, she scored the top grades in most of her classes. Malala also helped other girls to study. In addition, she pushed her father to provide free education to poor students.

Malala, her family, and most Pakistanis are Muslims. However, not all Muslims are the same. One minority group of Muslims, called the Taliban, don't want females studying, holding jobs, or walking freely. When Malala was 10, Taliban soldiers moved into the Swat Valley, which includes Mingora.

The Taliban destroyed over a hundred schools in the Swat Valley. They drove through the streets with machine guns. They **threatened** and violently punished those who did not obey them. Even policemen were killed.

The Taliban also threatened female school children and their teachers. Despite the threats, Malala's father contributed a short article in support of educating girls to a local newspaper. Malala also gave a speech in front of reporters from all over Pakistan. The title was "How Dare the Taliban Take Away My Basic Right to Education?"

The British Broadcasting Corporation (BBC) contacted Ziauddin. The BBC wanted someone to secretly write a blog about life under the Taliban. Malala agreed to write "Diary of a Pakistani schoolgirl." She wrote about studying, threats, and suicide bombings.

1
2
3
4
5
6
7
8
9
10
11
12
13
14
15
16
17
18
19
20
21
22
23
24
25
26
27
28
29
30
31
32

Because of fear, many girls and teachers stopped going to school. Despite the
danger, Malala spoke on a Pakistani talk show. Malala and her father also discussed
Pakistan and the Taliban's war on girls' education in an American media company's
documentary. People worldwide saw her face and listened to her brave words. She
said, "They cannot stop me. I will get my education, if it is in the home, school, or
anyplace." Malala became a famous **advocate** of education for females.

Not long afterward, the Taliban posted internet videos threatening her. Then, one
terrible day, a man got into the school bus she was riding home. He pointed a pistol
at her and shot 15-year-old Malala in the head. Then, all was dark.

When she regained awareness, she discovered she was in a British hospital.
Members of the Pakistani government worried that the Taliban might try again to
kill her. Malala and her family now live in England.

The United Nations requested Malala to speak at an international event, which
they later called Malala Day. It was her 16th birthday. She talked about peace, love,
and children's rights. That year, she also wrote a book about her fight for education.

One year afterward, she won the Nobel Peace Prize and half a million dollars for
advocating peace and education. But, instead of spending that money on herself, she
and her father founded the Malala Fund. This organization builds schools, advocates
for girls, and supports the work of future female leaders in numerous countries.

The Malala Fund's website includes this powerful message: "Let's not clip or
weaken the wings of women and girls, let's flourish and fly together."

Malala and her family at a press conference in Birmingham after the Nobel Peace Prize winner announcement on October 10, 2014

A What would be the best title for the passage?

    a. A Victim in Pakistan

    b. A Brave Advocate for Girls' Education

    c. Studying During a Time of War

    d. Pakistani Culture

B Write numbers to show the order of the events.

    __1__   Malala was born in Mingora.

    _____   She won a Nobel Peace Prize.

    _____   A member of the Taliban shot her.

    _____   The Taliban moved into the Swat Valley.

    _____   She secretly wrote a blog titled "Diary of a Pakistani schoolgirl."

    _____   She woke up in a hospital in the UK.

    __7__   She and her father founded the Malala Fund.

C Circle "C" for the correct information and "I" for the incorrect information. If the information is incorrect, revise the sentence.

    Ex. Malala Yousafzai was shot in the foot.

        [C /(I)]   _Malala Yousafzai was shot in the head._

    1. Malala was passionate about playing video games.

        [C / I]   _____

    2. Malala's father founded schools, and he encouraged her to study.

        [C / I]   _____

    3. Malala secretly wrote a blog about life in Pakistan for the NHK.

        [C / I]   _____

    4. The Taliban posted internet videos praising Malala.

        [C / I]   _____

5. Malala gave a speech for the United Nations.

[C / I] _____

6. The Malala Fund supports the work of future female leaders in numerous countries.

[C / I] _____

Listening

A Listen to the questions while scanning the passage and circle the best answers.

A
12-15

1. **a.** one **b.** two **c.** three **d.** four

2. **a.** nurse **b.** writer **c.** doctor **d.** school principal

3. **a.** chemistry **b.** peace **c.** medicine **d.** literature

4. **a.** the UK **b.** the US **c.** the UAE **d.** the BBC

B Listen to the story and complete the script below.

A
16

A Great Japanese Author

Higuchi Ichiyo's face is on five-_____-yen bills. She is famous for her

_____ poems, short stories, and novels that she _____ in her early

20s. Her actual name was Natsu, so Ichiyo is her pen _____. Her stories often

_____ on the lives of suffering women.

She _____ had a tough life. Higuchi

_____ early at the age of 24. Now, she

is considered one of the first _____

female writers of modern literature in Japan. Her

_____ still continue to inspire other

_____ writers today.

Higuchi Ichiyo's face on the bill

Your Own Ideas

A Match the questions with the answers.

1. In general, do female workers have the same rights as male workers? ___

2. If you were to blog about a global issue, what would you write about? ___

3. Who is a woman, besides Malala, that you admire and why? ___

4. Are you passionate about anything? If yes, what are you passionate about? ___

5. When will your country have its first female prime minister? ___

6. How do you feel about expressing your opinions in public? ___

a. Probably not. I have read that men usually receive higher salaries than women for the same job.

b. I need to develop the self-confidence to express my opinions.

c. I'm very passionate about expressing myself through art. Painting makes me feel great.

d. Chiaki Mukai is a woman I admire. She is a doctor, and she became Japan's first female astronaut.

e. Probably the problem of climate change because I'm very concerned about that.

f. Not in the next few years, but we might have one in the next decade.

B Work in pairs. Take turns asking the questions above and answering with your own ideas.

Critical Thinking

A Read each statement below and write your opinion using one of the five key phrases in the example.

> **Ex.** Men and women will soon have equal opportunities in our country.
>
> - **I strongly agree.** Women can study at all schools, and discrimination is illegal.
> - **I somewhat agree.** Discrimination is decreasing. Women can now more easily enter college than before, but discrimination won't disappear fast enough.
> - **I'm not sure.** I should learn more about this topic before I make a decision.
> - **I somewhat disagree.** Opportunities for women are increasing, but most national leaders are men. It will take another generation for society to change.
> - **I strongly disagree.** Japan has never had a female prime minister. Women are still paid less than men. The situation won't change for a long time.

1. Many women quit jobs to raise children, so women should be paid less than men.

   _____

2. Girls are naturally better students than boys.

   _____

3. Female high school student uniforms should include below-the-knee skirts.

   _____

B Share your opinions with your classmates.

Taking Action

▶ Follow the steps to take action.

| Step 1 | Research some websites introducing professional female workers. Then, choose a person to present about. |

| Step 2 | Prepare to give a timed presentation about the woman you chose. |

| Step 3 | In a small group, take turns giving presentations. |

Unit 3
Emotional Support

Parker Todd

Getting Ready

▶ Work in pairs. Look at the pictures and discuss the questions below.

1. Have you learned anything important from comic books or manga?

2. Which manga characters would be fun to meet?

3. Where are they? Why is the man dressed as a clown?

4. If you could create a comic book, what type of story would you tell?

Vocabulary

A Read the sentences and guess the meanings of the bold words.

A
18

1. The doctor said taking all of the medicine is **essential**.

2. The **compassionate** girl donated her birthday money to a charity that helps poor children.

3. Viruses can cause **diseases** such as influenza and COVID-19.

4. COVID-19 had a **tremendous** influence on hospitals. Thousands of healthcare workers became ill.

5. Doctors and nurses work hard to help their **patients**.

6. My mother was my **inspiration** to become a doctor. She gave me the idea and confidence to succeed.

7. The woman took care of her sick parents, worked all day, and studied at night. Despite such **hardships**, she became the leader of her country.

B Fill in the blanks with the bold words above. Change the form if necessary.

A
62

Ex. The man helped thousands of refugees when he was young. Today, he is an _inspiration_ for youth worldwide.

1. The manga artist turned off her phone and finished a _____ amount of work before quitting time.

2. Therapy dogs are trained to comfort _____ in hospitals and people in nursing homes.

3. The sudden loss of a job was a financial _____ for my sick brother.

4. Many young people cannot live without a phone. They think it is _____.

5. People who do not eat well and do not exercise might get _____ more often than people who take care of their health.

6. _____ individuals care about and try to improve the lives of others.

Reading

▶ Read the passage. Then, answer the following questions.

Parker Todd is a 12-year-old author of an **essential** and entertaining book about a serious topic. He is creative, generous, and **compassionate**, and he is also fighting sickle cell **disease**. It is a blood disease that causes **tremendous** pain and other health problems. People with this disease have trouble studying, enjoying sports, and working. Most **patients** with sickle cell disease cannot be cured. They must live with the pain and various other troubles.

Since he was a young child, Parker has been in and out of hospitals. While he was struggling with the pain of his disease, he met many other children fighting their own diseases, pain, and fears. After leaving the hospital, he couldn't stop thinking about those children.

At the age of 11, he decided to write a comic book about his experiences. When he turned 12, he finished and published his book, *The Adventures of the Sickler*. Parker says that he wrote the book to help other children overcome their problems. The hero of his book is a boy who helps other people by turning pain into power. The boy is a superhero who, while fighting his illness, wipes the tears off the faces of children in pain. Parker and his book give hope and power to many ill children.

Since the book was published, he has returned to hospitals, but not as a patient. Parker's positive attitude and good eating habits are helping him to stay healthy. He returns to hospitals to read his book aloud to younger children who are being treated for sickle cell disease, cancer, and other diseases. His book and his visits make them feel better.

Parker Todd has positively affected thousands of others. He is an **inspiration** for not just young, sick children, but for all of us. Despite his youth, he is an example of compassion, creativity, and courage. Parker is a spokesperson for children fighting diseases. After the publication of his book, television shows invited him to speak about how to deal with pain, stay positive, and be healthy.

He has a website that offers advice to children. His tips for other children are these: "Always think positive thoughts. Listen to your parents. Drink lots of water. Laugh out loud. Be kind to others." His last piece of advice is for children to read *The Adventures of the Sickler*.

Some people who suffer from terrible illnesses, injuries, and other **hardships** overcome their misfortunes. Psychologists use the phrase "post-traumatic growth"

1
2
3
4
5
6
7
8
9
10
11
12
13
14
15
16
17
18
19
20
21
22
23
24
25
26
27
28
29
30
31
32

to explain what drives people like Parker, to become advisors or counselors. Parker's 33
disease is painful, but he grew mentally and emotionally from his experiences. Now, 34
he is using what he learned to help other people. 35

Parker is unique, but the story of a person who has suffered and then begins 36
to help other people is not uncommon. However, we do not need to experience 37
misfortune before we help others. Many hospitals and nursing homes are full of 38
children and adults who need cheering up. Why not present them with the gift of 39
your time? They will feel better, and so will you. 40

Fourteen-year-old Parker autographing copies of *The Adventures of the Sickler*

A What would be the best title for the passage?

a. A Boy Fighting His Disease

b. An Ill Child Helping Others

c. Terrible Diseases around the World

d. Writing a Great Book

B Write numbers to show the order of the events.

_1_ Parker became sick when he was little.

____ He returned to hospitals to read his book aloud to younger children.

____ He decided to write a book.

____ His book was published.

____ He couldn't stop thinking about the sick children he had met.

____ Television shows asked him to come and speak.

_7_ Television viewers were inspired by him.

C Circle "C" for the correct information and "I" for the incorrect information. If the information is incorrect, revise the sentence.

Ex. Parker is the author of a novel.

[C / (I)] _Parker is the author of a comic book._

1. The illness that Parker has is called sickle cell disease.

[C / I] _____

2. Parker has been in and out of hospitals since he was a young man.

[C / I] _____

3. Parker has negatively affected thousands of other ill children.

[C / I] _____

4. Parker has a website that offers medicine to children.

[C / I] _____

5. Some people who suffer from serious illnesses overcome their misfortunes.

   [C / I] _____

6. Many children in hospitals and adults in nursing homes need cheering up.

   [C / I] _____

Listening

A Listen to the questions while scanning the passage and circle the best answers.

A
20-23

1. **a.** selfish   **b.** generous   **c.** caring   **d.** creative

2. **a.** makeup   **b.** smiles   **c.** dirt   **d.** tears

3. **a.** think positively   **b.** do homework   **c.** be kind   **d.** laugh a lot

4. **a.** emotionally   **b.** physically   **c.** slowly   **d.** negatively

B Listen to the story and complete the script below.

A
24

Illustrated Literature

What do the Bible, Shakespeare's plays,

_____ Keiji Nakazawa's *Barefoot Gen*

have in _____? All of these written works

have _____ millions of people. The

Bible and Shakespeare's plays weren't originally

_____ with many graphics. However,

modern publishers have _____ them

with manga-like _____ and easier-

to-understand vocabulary. All _____

works have serious lessons about _____

and morality. Teachers are using these to

_____ students about the past, in

the _____ that we will have a better

_____.

An illustrated page in a 13th-century edition of the New Testament

Portrait of Shakespeare and a scene from the play *Romeo and Juliet*

Your Own Ideas

A Match the questions with the answers.

A 63

1. What are some activities that you could do as a hospital volunteer? ___

2. Would you like to volunteer at a hospital or nursing home? ___

3. How could hospitals become more enjoyable places for sick people? ___

4. Are you usually a positive thinker? ___

5. Why do so many people like comic books or manga? ___

6. If you were a language teacher, would you use manga as teaching materials? ___

a. It's because many pictures help readers understand the story more clearly.

b. Reading books aloud, playing games with patients, and joining patients on walks are some volunteer activities I could do.

c. I'm positive most of the time.

d. Hospitals could have movie theaters and cafés with views of beautiful gardens.

e. Definitely. Helping sick people would be very rewarding.

f. Maybe yes. I'd use them for reading class, but not for teaching grammar.

B Work in pairs. Take turns asking the questions above and answering with your own ideas.

Critical Thinking

A Read each statement below and write your opinion using one of the five key phrases in the example.

A
25

Ex. Japanese colleges and high schools should provide lessons on manga in Japanese literature classes.

- **I strongly agree.** Manga is an aspect of our culture. We should understand it better so we can speak about manga with foreigners.
- **I somewhat agree.** Manga is definitely a part of Japanese culture, but not everyone needs to study it. Classes on manga could be elective.
- **I'm not sure.** I've never thought about this, and I don't care about manga.
- **I somewhat disagree.** Manga is entertaining, but teachers should focus on traditional literature instead.
- **I strongly disagree.** Manga is for children. Studying manga is a waste of time.

1. Doctors and nurses should receive the same salaries.

_____

2. Most schools are succeeding at teaching young people to be creative thinkers.

_____

3. A positive attitude can help people to recover from illnesses and injuries.

_____

B Share your opinions with your classmates.

Taking Action

▶ Follow the steps to take action.

Step 1	In a small group, choose a person to contact a volunteer coordinator at a local hospital and ask how students can help.
Step 2	The callers report on the conversations in class. Each group decides on one volunteer action to take.
Step 3	After volunteering, share your experience with other groups.

Poaching

Female Anti-poaching Rangers

Getting Ready

▶ Work in pairs. Look at the pictures and discuss the questions below.

1. These people are trying to move a rhinoceros to a safe place. Why?

2. Why do people hunt animals?

3. What is the purpose of this object?

4. How many of the animals above can you name in English?

Vocabulary

A Read the sentences and guess the meanings of the bold words.

1. Police discovered the people illegally taking plants and killing animals, and then arrested them for the crime of **poaching**.

2. About 4,000 tigers are living in the wild today. They are one of many **endangered** species that we must take action to protect.

3. The criminals who robbed the bank were **armed** with guns and knives.

4. The job duties of park **rangers** include protecting the plants, animals, and visitors within parks.

5. The police are **skeptical** of what others say because many people lie to them.

6. The hunter left a **snare** in the forest last night. When he returned this morning, he found a scared deer with its front right leg caught inside it.

7. Light punishments do not **deter** hunters from illegally killing animals. Heavy punishments do.

B Fill in the blanks with the bold words above. Change the form if necessary.

> **Ex.** I am _skeptical_ of politicians' promises to save wildlife and fight climate change.

1. My daughter loves wild animals and wants to save the environment. Her dream is to be a _____ in an African wildlife park.

2. Elephants are _____. They might all disappear soon.

3. Most of the police officers in the US are _____ with pistols.

4. _____ is a worldwide problem. The bodies of many animals are illegally sold for lots of money.

5. Because deer were eating his vegetables, the farmer used _____ to catch them.

6. The small warning sign is not enough to _____ tourists from feeding animals.

▶ Read the passage. Then, answer the following questions.

The **poaching** and the selling of wild animals and plants are illegal big-money businesses. Poaching is one of the major reasons why some species, such as elephants, rhinos, and pangolins, are **endangered**. Every year, poachers illegally kill and take millions of animals and plants.

Many poachers are **armed** with high-quality weapons. However, brave park **rangers** are taking action to stop poachers. Although their work is often dangerous, many park rangers are unarmed. Poachers are responsible for around two-thirds of ranger deaths.

Approximately half the poaching in the world happens in Africa, where all park rangers were male until 2013. Then, an NGO working with the South African government decided to form the world's first group of female anti-poaching rangers.

The beginning step was convincing local communities to accept this. Many South Africans were **skeptical** that women could successfully do what was traditionally the job of men. Women in the tribes around the park usually work as caregivers in their family homes. Finally, however, women applied for the job.

First, the applicants had to pass a tough three-month training program, including classes, fitness development, and survival training. Survival training included lessons on dealing with attacks from large animals such as lions or buffalos and learning how to follow and hide from poachers when necessary. Rangers need to be physically and mentally strong.

After passing the training program, their manager called the group of successful applicants the Black Mambas. "Black Mamba" is also the name of a species of aggressive and deadly snake. The female rangers work aggressively and effectively. While hiking through the park, they find and remove **snares** and search for signs of poachers. When the rangers discover poachers, they report their locations. Armed guards then attempt to arrest the poachers. The Black Mambas found almost two-thirds of the poachers arrested in their area of South Africa's Greater Kruger Park. The female rangers successfully **deter** many poachers. As a result, the poaching of many animals, including endangered rhinos, greatly decreased.

Besides searching for snares and poachers, the rangers also assist with the Bush Babies Environmental Education Program. They visit 13 schools in communities close to the park. Every week, they teach more than 1,300 children about the rangers'

1
2
3
4
5
6
7
8
9
10
11
12
13
14
15
16
17
18
19
20
21
22
23
24
25
26
27
28
29
30
31
32

experiences and the importance of protecting the natural heritage of South Africa. 33

The work of the first six Black Mambas members was so successful that the 34
government decided to add more members to the group. The number of rangers 35
climbed to 36. These female rangers have become international heroes and role 36
models. 37

Parks in other countries are also developing female ranger teams. For example, 38
Zimbabwe founded its first all-female anti-poaching group in 2017. This group 39
was named Akashinga, which translates as "brave ones." Unlike the Black Mambas, 40
Akashinga are armed. Their training is perhaps the most difficult of all the female 41
ranger groups. Akashinga learn to fight and survive in the wild, just like soldiers. 42

Two years later, Kenya founded Team Lioness. The newest all-female ranger unit 43
was recently created in Zambia. The name is Kufadza, meaning "inspire." These two 44
ranger groups are unarmed. 45

Many of the rangers come from poor families. Their work as rangers helps them 46
protect the natural world, buy property, pay for their children's education, and make 47
a better future for boys and girls. 48

The female rangers set great examples for young men and women. Supporters 49
of these inspirational women celebrated the first World Female Ranger Day on June 50
23, 2021. It is a day to show appreciation and support for female rangers. Currently, 51
around 11 percent of the world's rangers are females. May there be many more! 52

Left: Rangers of the Black Mambas are removing a snare during their
patrol. Poachers usually attach one end to a tree. Then, they bend the
other end into a loop that can trap animals by their necks or legs.
Right: A snare is made with a piece of wire. The more a trapped animal
moves, the tighter the looped part becomes.

A What would be the best title for the passage?

    a. Female Rangers Stopping Poaching

    b. Female Poachers and Park Rangers

    c. Environmental Issues in Africa

    d. Living with Wild Animals

B Write numbers to show the order of the events.

    __1__   All rangers in Africa were men.

    _____   People were skeptical about female rangers in South Africa.

    _____   Team Lioness was created in Kenya.

    _____   The Black Mambas grew into a larger group of rangers.

    _____   Zimbabwe started its own all-female anti-poaching group.

    _____   The Black Mambas was founded.

    __7__   World Female Ranger Day was first celebrated on June 23, 2021.

C Circle "C" for the correct information and "I" for the incorrect information. If the information is incorrect, revise the sentence.

    Ex. The Black Mambas is a group of male park rangers.

        [C /(I)]   *The Black Mambas is a group of female park rangers.*

1. Poachers illegally kill and take thousands of animals and plants each year.

    [C / I]   _____

2. The three-month training included classes, fitness development, and survival training.

    [C / I]   _____

3. The number of Black Mambas members climbed to 36.

    [C / I]   _____

4. Female rangers have become international heroes and fashion models.

    [C / I]   _____

5. Akashinga learn to fight and survive in the wild, just like soldiers.

[C / I] _____

6. The rangers set great examples for young women only.

[C / I] _____

Listening

A Listen to the questions while scanning the passage and circle the best answers.

1. **a.** low quality **b.** high quality **c.** unusual **d.** traditional
2. **a.** Team Lioness **b.** The Black Mambas **c.** Akashinga **d.** Kufadza
3. **a.** snares and poachers **b.** armed guards **c.** weapons **d.** large animals
4. **a.** 5 percent **b.** 11 percent **c.** 20 percent **d.** 34 percent

B Listen to the story and complete the script below.

Adventurous Environmentalist

Holly Budge is a tireless and _____ adventurer, designer, and conservationist. She _____ the first woman to skydive over Mt. Everest and has _____ to the summit. Holly also _____ 1,000 kilometers across Mongolia by _____ in nine days. Her next _____ is to hike nearly 5,000 kilometers of _____ Great Wall. Holly also founded an _____ named How Many Elephants. This organization _____ African elephants. Holly recently launched _____ Female Ranger Week and made a film _____ the Black Mambas.

On the summit of Mt. Everest, Holly holds a flag of How Many Elephants.

Your Own Ideas

A Match the questions with the answers.

1. If you could save one endangered animal species, which would you choose? Why? ____

2. Why should we care about the disappearance of animal species? ____

3. What is one positive and negative point of the work of female rangers? ____

4. What would you do if you could travel to Africa? ____

5. Which endangered animal species can you name? ____

6. What is your hometown, and can you see wild animals there? ____

a. A positive point is being able to save animals. A negative point is that their work can be dangerous.

b. I think that all animals are connected. If we lose more animals, our lives will be negatively affected.

c. I would save elephants because I have read that they are intelligent and loving animals.

d. I'm from Yuzawa, Niigata. I sometimes see deer, monkeys, and raccoon dogs.

e. I would visit parks to see wildlife and try different foods.

f. African tigers, the Tsushima leopard cat, and polar bears are endangered.

B Work in pairs. Take turns asking the questions above and answering with your own ideas.

Critical Thinking

A Read each statement below and write your opinion using one of the five key phrases in the example.

Ex. Poachers should be severely punished with long prison sentences.

- **I strongly agree.** Poaching is a terrible crime against both humankind and nature. Strong punishments are necessary to deter poachers.
- **I somewhat agree.** Poaching is terrible, but maybe first-time poachers should get easier punishments than second-time poachers.
- **I'm not sure.** I don't know if that will deter or not deter poachers.
- **I somewhat disagree.** Poaching is wrong, but some poor poachers do it to feed their families. They should not have very long prison sentences.
- **I strongly disagree.** Long prison sentences do not deter poachers. Instead, we should help them to find different jobs.

---

1. We should use cloning techniques to bring extinct species back to life.

   _____

2. Schools should take students to study wildlife in parks instead of visiting cities.

   _____

3. Saving wild animals and plants is more important than saving cats and dogs.

   _____

B Share your opinions with your classmates.

Taking Action

▶ Follow the steps to take action.

Step 1 〉	Research some NPOs that protect endangered animal species. Then, choose the one you believe does the most valuable work and write a short summary.
Step 2 〉	In a small group, read your summaries and choose the one you want to help.
Step 3 〉	Think of an action you can take to help the organization. You might collect money or goods and donate what you collect.

Unit 5
Reforestation

Jadav Payeng

Getting Ready

▶ **Work in pairs. Look at the pictures and discuss the questions below.**

1. Do you enjoy walking in forests? Why or why not?

2. What are the benefits of planting trees?

3. What will probably happen to the animals that lived here?

4. Besides bears, what are some animals that live in forests in your country?

Vocabulary

A Read the sentences and guess the meanings of the bold words.

A
34

1. We should plant trees to **reforest** areas where trees were cut or burned.

2. This area used to have thousands of trees, but they were all cut. The land was **deforested**.

3. Most squirrels need trees for food and homes. Forests are their **habitats**.

4. Environmental **activists** work very hard to save the natural world.

5. Much more rain than normal fell. Then, a **flood** destroyed farms and homes.

6. The drought and fire killed all the plants and animals. The land is **lifeless**.

7. I studied **forestry** in college. Now, I work to keep forests healthy.

B Fill in the blanks with the bold words above. Change the form if necessary.

A
66

Ex. The _habitat_ of polar bears is too cold for gorillas.

1. The construction of a dam stopped water from flowing downriver. As a result, all the animals died and the river became _____.

2. It rained so much that the river could not hold all the water. As a result, homes and lives were lost in the terrible _____.

3. We cannot find birds called woodpeckers on this _____ mountain. These birds need trees to live.

4. To increase the population of wild animals, we could _____ the areas of farmland that no one uses anymore.

5. After I graduate, I will become an _____ who works to make the world a better place for animals, plants, and people.

6. I saw some _____ workers planting trees in the national park.

Reading

▶ Read the passage. Then, answer the following questions.

Jadav working to grow plants in Northern Assam, India

Jadav Payeng was born into a low-income family in a remote area in Northern Assam, India. He became world-famous after the news spread that Jadav had **reforested** a treeless area of 5.5-square-kilometers. His efforts turned a **deforested** region into a healthy **habitat** for snakes, rhinos, tigers, elephants, and more. People call him "The Forest Man of India."

His path toward becoming an environmental **activist** started with his decision to grow a forest when he was 16 in 1979. Near his home, villagers and timber companies were cutting large numbers of trees for timber and fuel. Without tree roots to hold soil in place during heavy rains, the earth along the sides of hills and rivers was sliding away. As a result, homes, temples, and farms were falling into the rivers.

After one destructive rainstorm and **flood**, Jadav took a walk to see the damage. On a treeless island in a big river, he found many dead snakes and other animals. During the flood, those animals had swum to the treeless island for safety. However, without shade, the animals died beneath the hot sun after the rain stopped. With tears in his eyes, Jadav knew he had to take action.

He asked local government forest department officers to plant trees on the riverside. They said that trees could not grow in that **lifeless** area and suggested that he plant bamboo.

Jadav moved to the riverside, lived in a hut, and started growing bamboo. He carried bamboo roots to the island, planted the roots in holes that he dug, and watered the bamboo with buckets. He repeated this process for days and months. Within a few years, the bamboo forest was tall and thick.

After that, Jadav decided to grow trees and other plants along the riverside. He had never studied biology or **forestry**, but Jadav observed and learned from nature. Realizing that soil needs insects to be healthy, he caught red ants and other insects.

He carried them to his growing forest. Although the insects bit him and the work was 33
hard, he never quit. 34

Years turned into decades. Researchers estimate that Jadav was responsible for 35
the growth of tens of millions of plants. His efforts turned the lifeless ground into a 36
healthy forest that naturally continued growing. After birds brought seeds into the 37
woods, the size and the varieties of plants increased. Deer and wild cattle settled in 38
the woods. Jadav discovered tigers and even a rhino. Probably those animals were 39
searching for a safe place to live after humans had destroyed their previous habitats. 40

Jadav is willing to defend the reforested land and its creatures from anyone who 41
tries to kill animals or remove plants. He tells poachers and loggers that he will fight 42
to the death to protect the forest. 43

In 2008, almost 30 years after Jadav decided to save animals and plants, 44
government forestry officials who were studying elephants discovered his forest. 45
The forestry officials were amazed that one man could restore a forest. 46

After that, Jadav received many awards and praise from around the world. In 47
2020, the Mexican government requested his help with a project to grow 7,000,000 48
trees. Jadav plans to continue with his lifework. His example teaches us that 49
reforesting treeless and lifeless lands is something we can all do. 50

Jadav was photographed on October 27, 2013, in the large forest he created.

A What would be the best title for the passage?

    a. How Governments Protect Forests

    b. One Person Helping Forests Recover

    c. Saving the Earth Together

    d. Awards for Planting Trees

B Write numbers to show the order of the events.

    __1__   Jadav was born in a remote area in India.

    _____   He decided to plant trees.

    _____   He started growing bamboo.

    _____   He was upset after seeing dead animals after a flood.

    _____   Indian government workers discovered elephants in his forest.

    _____   He became world-famous for his efforts to reforest.

    __7__   The Mexican government asked for his advice.

C Circle "C" for the correct information and "I" for the incorrect information. If the information is incorrect, revise the sentence.

    Ex. Jadav started his reforesting project by growing coconut trees.

        [C /(I)]   *Jadav started his reforesting project by growing bamboo.*

    1. Tree leaves hold soil in place during heavy rains.

        [C / I] _____

    2. Many animals died on an island because there were no trees.

        [C / I] _____

    3. Jadav observed and learned from scientists.

        [C / I] _____

    4. Researchers estimate that Jadav was responsible for the growth of tens of millions of plants.

        [C / I] _____

5. Forestry officials were amazed that one man could destroy a forest.

[C / I] _____

6. The government of Mexico requested Jadav's help with deforestation.

[C / I] _____

Listening

A Listen to the questions while scanning the passage and circle the best answers.

A
36-39

1. **a.** 6   **b.** 16   **c.** 26   **d.** 60

2. **a.** in a forest   **b.** on a riverside   **c.** on a hill   **d.** on an island

3. **a.** seeds   **b.** eggs   **c.** feathers   **d.** insects

4. **a.** only India   **b.** around Asia   **c.** around the world   **d.** just Mexico

B Listen to the story and complete the script below.

A
40

Kids Planting Trees

Felix Finkbeiner believes that young people _____ plant trees to reduce climate change. _____ a teenager, he organized over _____ children around the world to _____ millions of trees. At the age of 20, Felix started leading an international _____ to plant 1,000,000,000 trees.

Now, he _____ kids in each country to plant _____. He thinks taking _____ is more _____ than discussing problems. His motto is "Stop talking, _____ planting."

Felix poses next to a young tree in Germany on July 26, 2014. "Plant for the Planet" is printed on his T-shirt.

Your Own Ideas

A Match the questions with the answers.

1. How are trees used after they are cut into pieces? ___

2. Where would be some good places to grow trees in your town? ___

3. What are some environmental problems in your area of Japan? ___

4. Have you ever grown plants or taken care of animals? ___

5. What are the names of wild animals you see around your area? ___

6. If you had your own land, what would you plant? Why? ___

a. I would plant colorful native flowers. They are pretty and feed butterflies.

b. They are used for lumber, paper, and fuel.

c. We have too much rain these days, but in winter, less snow falls than before.

d. Tall trees in the center of town would be great. They would provide shade.

e. I see crows in shrines and dragonflies around the cabbage fields.

f. Yes. I help my parents grow vegetables. And I had a dog when I was a child.

B Work in pairs. Take turns asking the questions above and answering with your own ideas.

Critical Thinking

A Read each statement below and write your opinion using one of the five key phrases in the example.

Ex. Japanese people should stop using disposable wooden chopsticks.

- **I strongly agree.** Throwing away chopsticks after using them just once is a waste of a natural resource.
- **I somewhat agree.** Reusable chopsticks are often eco-friendlier than disposable ones, but homemade ones made from branches are OK.
- **I'm not sure.** There are both positive and negative points to using disposable chopsticks.
- **I somewhat disagree.** Wooden chopsticks can be recycled into paper.
- **I strongly disagree.** We need to cut some trees to protect forests and most disposable chopsticks are made from that wood. Using them is not a problem.

1. Animals that enter farming areas should be killed.

2. City parks should have food and medicinal plants instead of decorative ones.

3. Cities should require all new buildings to have solar panels or gardens on the roofs.

B Share your opinions with your classmates.

Taking Action

▶ Follow the steps to take action.

Step 1 Research some tree-planting organizations. Then, choose the one you believe does the most valuable work and write a short summary about it.

Step 2 In a small group, read your summaries and choose the one you want to help.

Step 3 Think of an action you can take to help the organization. Otherwise, organize your own planting event and carry it out with your schoolmates.

Unit **6**

Bullying

Emily-Anne Rigal

Getting Ready

▶ Work in pairs. Look at the pictures and discuss the questions below.

1. Did you see students bullying others in the schools you attended?

2. Why do some people send mean messages to others?

3. Besides schools, where does the problem of bullying happen?

4. Who do you talk to when you have personal problems?

Vocabulary

A Read the sentences and guess the meanings of the bold words.

1. **Bullies** try to physically or emotionally hurt others.

2. The **victims** of the attack were taken to the hospital.

3. People with **self-confidence** tend to like themselves and are not afraid to express their opinions in front of others.

4. The mafia use violence to scare people to get what they want. In other words, they **terrorize** others.

5. After many students refused to speak to the new student, the teacher told them to stop **ignoring** him.

6. My counselor says that thinking about what I did would help me to understand myself. So, I try to **reflect** on my behavior at the end of each day.

7. I can **relate** to your suffering since I have had similar painful experiences.

B Fill in the blanks with the bold words above. Change the form if necessary.

Ex. After I fought with my sister, my mother put us in separate rooms and told us to
reflect on our actions.

1. Many school _____ are children who were hurt before, sometimes at home.

2. The older students _____ me so much that I was shaking from fear after they left.

3. I want my children to grow mentally strong and study karate, so they will not become _____.

4. Although I am American and you are Japanese, we are both parents, so I can _____ to your worries.

5. Because I lacked _____, I rarely spoke up in class.

6. Please spend time with unpopular students. Do not _____ them.

▶ Read the passage. Then, answer the following questions.

A
43

Bullying is a global problem. Stories of **bullies** and their **victims** often make the   1
front pages of newspapers in Japan. Not too long ago, The Asahi Shimbun published   2
a shocking article about bullying. According to that 2020 story, over 82% of schools   3
in Japan had at least one case of bullying. In 2019, the government recorded 612,496   4
cases of bullying. The victims suffered physically and emotionally.   5

Of course, government leaders and school officials are trying to tackle bullying.   6
But in some cases, victims of bullying and their friends are creating their own   7
solutions.   8

One of many examples is Emily-Anne Rigal. First, she was a nine-year-old victim.   9
Then, she turned into a bully. Finally, she became an anti-bullying activist.   10

Today, she shares her story through videos, a new book, conferences, and   11
magazine articles. Her problems, she says, started in elementary school. Other   12
students made fun of her because Emily-Anne was overweight, unathletic, and uncool.   13
They did not invite her to play games and insulted her. She lost her **self-confidence**.   14

As time passed, students **terrorized** her so much that she wandered alone   15
through the school halls staring at the ground. Emily-Anne told an interviewer that   16
she feared students would repeatedly call her fat and ugly or **ignore** her. Only a few   17
students insulted her, but many students ignored her. Those students did not want   18
to be seen with an uncool victim. It was too much for her, so she moved to another   19
school.   20

The new school was an opportunity for a fresh start. She made friends, but she   21
still lacked self-confidence. Emily-Anne was afraid of becoming a victim again, so she   22
started acting like a bully, ignoring and insulting other girls.   23

One of her new friends eventually made her **reflect** on her behavior. Emily-Anne   24
regretted hurting others. She decided to be a better person, stop bullying others, and   25
apologize to her victims.   26

As she spent more time being a good friend to others, her self-confidence grew.   27
So did her creativity. With her friends, she made funny YouTube videos under the   28
name Schmiddlebopper. The videos became extremely popular.   29

Then, at the age of 16, she decided to tackle bullying with YouTube videos. She   30
created a YouTube channel that she named WeStopHate. Emily-Anne and her other   31
teenage friends created a series of videos on the topic of bullying. They told their   32

stories about being bullied. Within less than one year, WeStopHate became one of 33
the top non-profit YouTube channels. Teenagers across the world **related** to their 34
experiences. Her channel soon had over one million views. As a result, she won a 35
HALO Award. These awards are for teenagers who have taken action to change the 36
world for the better. 37

Not long afterward, Lady Gaga invited Emily-Anne to speak about WeStopHate 38
on an MTV show. Since then, Emily-Anne has given many public speeches and has 39
written a book titled *Flawd* about her experiences. 40

Perhaps, the most essential piece of advice that she tells others is to speak up 41
about bullying. She explains that bullied students should not be ashamed to ask for 42
help. The advice she offers in her videos, speeches, and *Flawd* has helped victims of 43
bullying around the world. 44

Emily-Anne did not give specific advice regarding where students in Japan can go 45
for help. In Japan, Japanese-language assistance is available on the webpage of the 46
Ministry of Justice. And students who need English-language support can find it on 47
the webpage of the Tokyo English Lifeline (TELL), an NPO that provides counseling 48
to foreign residents in Japan. 49

Upper: Emily-Anne and other winners during the HALO Awards held at the Hollywood Palladium on October 26, 2011
Lower: Emily-Anne on stage with television host Nick Cannon

A What would be the best title for the passage?

   a. Improving Schools

   b. Punishing the Bullies

   c. Why do Bullies Hurt Others?

   d. Overcoming Bullying

B Write numbers to show the order of the events.

   _1_   Emily-Anne was insulted in elementary school.

   ____   She reflected on her behavior and stopped bullying.

   ____   She founded WeStopHate.

   ____   Because she was terrorized by students, she changed schools.

   ____   She bullied other girls.

   ____   Teenagers around the world related to her experiences.

   _7_   *Flawd* was published.

C Circle "C" for the correct information and "I" for the incorrect information. If the information is incorrect, revise the sentence.

   Ex. Less than 82% of Japanese schools had at least one case of bullying.

   [C /Ⓘ]   *Over 82% of Japanese schools had at least one case of bullying.*

1. Emily-Anne was an athletic student in elementary school.

   [C / I]   _____

2. Emily-Anne was a victim and a bully, but now she is an anti-bullying activist.

   [C / I]   _____

3. In elementary school, Emily-Anne used to look up at the ceilings.

   [C / I]   _____

4. Emily-Anne and her friends made a series of books about the topic of bullying.

   [C / I]   _____

5. Emily-Anne was 16 years old when she started WeStopHate.

[C / I] _____

6. Emily-Anne's advice is not to speak up about bullying.

[C / I] _____

Listening

A Listen to the questions while scanning the passage and circle the best answers.

1. **a.** solutions **b.** ignorance **c.** victims **d.** experiences
2. **a.** 9 **b.** 19 **c.** 16 **d.** 26
3. **a.** bullies **b.** a new school **c.** awards **d.** self-confidence
4. **a.** children **b.** teenagers **c.** young adults **d.** the elderly

B Listen to the story and complete the script below.

Developing Self Love

When she was in the seventh _____, Sanah Jivani suffered from hair loss. _____ that, bullying became a daily experience. _____ lost self-confidence and began to _____ herself. But after reflecting on her _____, she became happy by telling herself _____ messages and taking action to change _____ school. With like-minded students, she _____ events called Anti-bullying Week, The International _____ of Self Love, and Random _____ of Kindness Week. During this week, she _____ us to do many kind things for _____.

Sanah photographed on April 15, 2022, at Burnside Farms in Virginia, USA

Your Own Ideas

Match the questions with the answers.

1. What would you do if you were being bullied by a coworker? ____

2. If you could make videos to help others, what topics would you choose? ____

3. Why do some victims of bullying not ask for help? ____

4. Did your high school classes ever cover the topic of bullying? ____

5. What would you do if you had a child and the child was bullied? ____

6. Have you learned anything interesting or important by watching YouTube videos? ____

a. I have learned a lot about different cultures by watching YouTube videos.

b. I'm not sure. Maybe they feel ashamed.

c. I would talk to another coworker or the manager.

d. I would make videos about my local area to attract tourists to visit and boost the economy.

e. I can't remember much. I think it was a topic that came up a few times when we studied current events.

f. I would get really angry and talk to the school principal or the bully's parents.

B Work in pairs. Take turns asking the questions above and answering with your own ideas.

Critical Thinking

A Read each statement below and write your opinion using one of the five key phrases in the example.

A
49

Ex. Teachers are completely responsible for solving bullying at school.

- **I strongly agree.** Most bullying happens at schools. Teachers can control the behavior of students.
- **I somewhat agree.** Teachers can solve the bullying problem, but only if parents help, too.
- **I'm not sure.** I honestly don't know who is responsible for solving this problem.
- **I somewhat disagree.** Teachers could reduce this problem a little, but parents should raise their children properly before starting school.
- **I strongly disagree.** Only bullies and their parents are responsible for this problem and solving it.

1. The Japanese government needs to create more anti-bullying posters.

_____

2. Bullies should be physically punished to change their mean behaviors.

_____

3. All governments should make hate speech on SNS illegal.

_____

B Share your opinions with your classmates.

Taking Action

▶ Follow the steps to take action.

Step 1	Create a kindness calendar for one week. Each day must include kindness goals like praising two friends, helping a stranger, or giving someone gifts.
Step 2	Each day of the next week, reach your kindness action goals.
Step 3	Later, report to your class what you did and how people reacted to your kindness.

Unit 7
Food Waste

Rayner Loi

Getting Ready

▶ Work in pairs. Look at the pictures and discuss the questions below.

1. How do you feel about eating vegetables and fruits that look unusual?

2. Many customers waste food when they are at all-you-can-eat buffets. Why?

3. How often do you or your family throw food away? Why?

4. Do you know what your school cafeteria does with uneaten food?

Vocabulary

A Read the sentences and guess the meanings of the bold words.

1. It is possible to **generate** fuel for cars with leftover vegetable oil.

2. The **starving** children will soon die unless the UN can bring food quickly.

3. Many people do not **utilize** all plant parts, but I try to do that. I always cook the leaves and seeds of the pumpkins from my garden.

4. People with low salaries face **food insecurity**. Each day they wonder if they will have enough food to be healthy.

5. Few people will eat vegetables or fruits that do not look beautiful, but this **ugly** food is often healthy and delicious.

6. **Nose-to-tail** cooking is more common in undeveloped countries than in modernized ones. In some areas, people eat the heads, meat, and tails of pigs.

7. My family always puts leftover food in a container in the garden. After a while, the food becomes good **compost** that we mix into the soil for the plants.

B Fill in the blanks with the bold words above. Change the form if necessary.

> **Ex.** The plants in our garden produce bigger vegetables because of the _compost_ we make with leftovers.

1. Let's not _____ any food waste from our party tomorrow!

2. _____ food preparation is not so popular in some cultures. Those people won't eat fish eyes or fish bones.

3. Orange peels can be _____ as a cleanser for kitchen plates.

4. Some cucumbers from my garden are _____, but they taste great.

5. Recent data shows that around 15 percent of Japanese people experience _____. Some students go to school hungry.

6. Because of the war, farmers cannot get to their farms, and people are _____.

Reading

▶ Read the passage. Then, answer the following questions.

A
51

Officials of the United Nations (UN) report that we waste half of all vegetables   1
and fruits, about 20 percent of animal meat and dairy products, and almost one-third   2
of fish every year. Food waste is a global problem. Japan **generates** 25 million tons   3
of food waste each year.   4

UN documents also inform us that worldwide almost one in three people (2.37   5
billion) did not have access to adequate food in 2020. In some places, people are   6
starving. In other areas, people do not die, but their health suffers, and they often   7
feel hungry.   8

Where is food being wasted? Unfortunately, the answer is that almost all farms,   9
factories, restaurants, grocery stores, and homes where food items are produced,   10
stored, and eaten are not **utilizing** food products well.   11

The problems of food waste, **food insecurity**, climate change, excessive garbage,   12
pollution, and deforestation are connected. If we learn to stop wasting food, more   13
food will be available at lower prices for everyone. Packaged food that is thrown   14
away adds to garbage problems, and rotting food releases methane, a greenhouse   15
gas. As the world population increases and food is wasted, people cut forests down   16
to make more farms.   17

Food waste is a severe problem, but it is one that we can reduce and solve by   18
taking some easy actions in our homes, workplaces, and schools. Lately, the issue   19
of food waste has been receiving global attention, and people are finding solutions.   20
Some of the actions to utilize and reduce food waste involve new technologies, and   21
some steps are ones that used to be customary, but are not followed much today.   22

Rayner Loi, a 22-year-old Singaporean college student, learned about food   23
insecurity in Singapore when he treated a younger student to dinner. Afterward, the   24
boy's mother cried, thanked him, and explained that they did not have dinner each   25
day. Rayner was shocked. Then, he started reading about food insecurity and food   26
waste.   27

With the assistance of another technologically skillful student, he created an AI   28
system to analyze the waste at buffets. Each evening, a computer that has learned to   29
identify food items scans and measures all the wasted food. The system provides the   30
restaurant management with information. For example, five kilograms of chicken   31
curry goes into the garbage every day, or lots of people take but do not finish   32

pieces of strawberry cake. In response, chefs might cook less chicken curry, and the restaurant might stop serving the unpopular cake variety. One restaurant manager said that his restaurant generated 20 percent less waste after trying Rayner's system. Now restaurants in many countries are interested in utilizing his system.

Before globalization and large supermarkets started providing us with packaged foods from all over the world, we used more food items around us. For example, long ago in tuna fishing areas, people ate every part of the fish, but today many cooks throw the skin, heart, and liver away. Nowadays, many people do not eat the leaves of daikon, but they are delicious when cooked well. Modern chefs are revisiting old recipes and creating new ones that use most parts of animals and plants, even the **ugly** ones. **Nose-to-tail** cooking is growing in popularity in Europe and North America. American chef Steven Satterfield wrote a popular cookbook titled *Root to Leaf*. He teaches other cooks to use all parts of vegetables. This style of cooking is called root-to-leaf cooking.

We can all take action to stop or reduce food waste at home. One easy idea is to put the older food items in the front of our refrigerators. Another is to learn to cook soups and other dishes with leftovers and food scraps. Also, food can become garden **compost** that helps to grow more food. A little research will teach you more ways to make the most of your food.

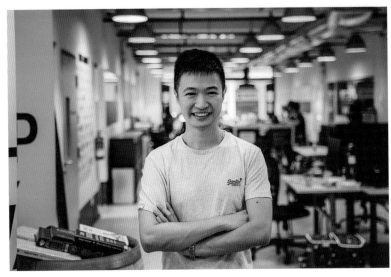

Rayner was photographed at Lumitics, the company that sells his food-waste-management solution.

A What would be the best title for the passage?

    a. Restaurant and Home Cooking

    b. New Ways of Storing Food

    c. Eating More Nutritious Food

    d. Reducing and Using Food Waste

B Write numbers to show the order of the events.

   _1_   Rayner took a younger student to dinner.

   ____   He was shocked that food insecurity is an issue in Singapore.

   ____   With another student, he created an AI system for reducing food waste.

   ____   He began to study food insecurity and food waste.

   ____   A restaurant reduced food waste after trying his system.

   ____   A mother told him that her family suffered from food insecurity.

   _7_   Now, restaurants in many countries are interested in his system.

C Circle "C" for the correct information and "I" for the incorrect information. If the information is incorrect, revise the sentence.

Ex. Japan generates 25 thousand tons of food waste each year.

    [C /(I)]   _Japan generates 25 million tons of food waste each year._

1. One-quarter of the world's population did not have adequate food in 2020.

    [C / I]   _____

2. Before globalization, people used more food items around them.

    [C / I]   _____

3. One easy action is to put the older food items in the back of refrigerators.

    [C / I]   _____

4. The leaves of daikon taste delicious when cooked well.

    [C / I]   _____

5. Nose-to-tail cooking is growing in popularity in Europe and North Asia.

[C / I]   _____

6. The AI system works to help restaurants generate food waste.

[C / I]   _____

Listening

A Listen to the questions while scanning the passage and circle the best answers.

A
52-55

1.   **a.** 50 percent   **b.** 30 percent   **c.** 20 percent   **d.** 10 percent

2.   **a.** wild animals   **b.** forests   **c.** factories   **d.** lakeside resorts

3.   **a.** around the world   **b.** in Europe   **c.** in the US   **d.** in Singapore

4.   **a.** nose-to-tail   **b.** seed-to-fruit   **c.** root-to-leaf   **d.** old-fashioned

B Listen to the story and complete the script below.

A
56

Food Scrap Chef

A young British chef, Shane Jordan, is becoming well _____ for his creative ways to reduce _____ waste and help feed those suffering from food _____ in the UK. He wrote a book _____ *Food Waste Philosophy*. He explains why he cares so _____ about helping other people and _____ food waste in that book. The book also contains _____ recipes for using _____ and food scraps. For _____, one recipe is for making curry _____ banana peels.

Shane volunteers at Food Cycle, which prepares healthy meals made from unwanted food for people in need.

63

Your Own Ideas

A Match the questions with the answers.

1. Can you tell me about your experience of wasting food? ___

2. What can people do with moldy cheese or hard bread? ___

3. What groups of people in Japan might suffer from food insecurity? ___

4. What do you think about volunteering at a food bank? ___

5. Would you buy ugly fruits or vegetables if stores sold them at lower prices? ___

6. What are the positive and negative points of buffet restaurants? ___

a. I took too much food at the all-you-can-eat restaurant. Then, I left half of the food on my plate.

b. The good points are that we can try different dishes and eat a lot for a reasonable price. On the other hand, people eat too much and restaurants throw away a lot.

c. Maybe old people on fixed incomes and single-parent families.

d. That's a great activity, but I don't have time. I can donate a little money or food, though.

e. Definitely. They are still good to eat, and I could save money.

f. We can cut the mold off the cheese and eat the good part. We can soak the hard bread in hot soup.

B Work in pairs. Take turns asking the questions above and answering with your own ideas.

Critical Thinking

A Read each statement below and write your opinion using one of the five key phrases in the example.

A
57

Ex. Students from elementary school to college should receive government-provided breakfasts and lunches.

- **I strongly agree.** All students would be healthier and could concentrate more.
- **I somewhat agree.** I think that free lunches should be provided, but it would be too expensive to also provide breakfasts.
- **I'm not sure.** I have never thought about this topic, and I can't decide now.
- **I somewhat disagree.** I don't think it's the government's responsibility to provide meals for everyone. Only food-insecure students should get free meals.
- **I strongly disagree.** It's not a government responsibility to feed students. That is the responsibility of their parents only.

1. Buffet restaurant customers who leave food on their plates should pay a fee.

_____

2. All restaurants and grocery stores should donate unsold foods to food banks.

_____

3. The government should make reducing food waste a national priority.

_____

B Share your opinions with your classmates.

Taking Action

▶ Follow the steps to take action.

Step 1 〉 In a small group, make a list of food and drink items we often throw away, such as tea bags, broccoli stems, apple cores, and coffee grinds.

Step 2 〉 Choose one item and research at least two ways to cook or use that item.

Step 3 〉 Share your research in class. Then, discuss ways to keep reducing your food waste at home.

Climate Change

Greta Thunberg

Getting Ready

▶ Work in pairs. Look at the pictures and discuss the questions below.

1. Do you think that human activities are causing global warming?

2. Why are these people demonstrating?

3. What does "There is no planet B" probably mean?

4. Which of your daily activities release greenhouse gases?

Vocabulary

A Read the sentences and guess the meanings of the bold words. B 02

1. Although very intelligent, she communicates and socializes differently than the average person. Doctors call her condition **Asperger's syndrome**.

2. The **carbon footprint**, or amount of greenhouse gases, released by a rich country is usually much larger than that of a poor country.

3. Healthy food, naps, and my friends **energize** me. They give me the power I need to continue as an environmental activist.

4. A large number of students decided not to go to school on Friday. The media wrote many stories about the school **strike**.

5. **Blunt** speakers express opinions without worrying about being polite.

6. When speaking at demonstrations, she **focuses** on presenting the information that is most likely to motivate the listeners.

7. Every year, many writers are **nominated** for the Nobel Prize in Literature, but usually, only one person gets the prize.

B Fill in the blanks with the bold words above. Change the form if necessary. B 58

Ex. Children with *Asperger's syndrome* can accomplish great things and help society.

1. The film *I Am Greta* was _____ for best documentary movie of the year.

2. Some people think his _____ communication style is rude.

3. An airplane has a larger _____ than a train.

4. The documentary about the loss of wildlife touched and _____ the students to start a school club to protect plants and animals.

5. The workers said their _____ would continue until they receive higher salaries and better conditions.

6. Mom says I must _____ on studying instead of joining protests.

▶ Read the passage. Then, answer the following questions.

Fifteen-year-old Greta, on August 28, 2018, sits with the sign "School Strike for Climate."

On January 3, 2003, Greta Thunberg was born in Stockholm, Sweden. Her parents never expected their daughter to become the world's most famous teenage environmental activist.

Greta first learned that climate change was causing floods, animals to go extinct, and people to become refugees when she was around eight years old. After that, she could not stop worrying about the world's future. Greta became so depressed for several years that she stopped speaking and barely ate.

Doctors told her parents that she had **Asperger's syndrome**. The family discussed her worries about climate change. When Greta was 12, she chose to stop flying on airplanes and eating meat. Her parents decided to travel less and eat less meat to reduce their **carbon footprint**. Her success in influencing her parents to become environmentally friendly **energized** Greta.

She decided to stop going to school on Fridays at the age of 15. Instead, she sat alone outside the Swedish parliament building, where politicians meet. While holding a sign that read "School **Strike** for Climate" in Swedish, she handed out leaflets to explain her protest. Many people criticized her. Strangers told her to be a good student and return to school. Nonetheless, she continued to strike every Friday. Soon others joined her strike.

Reporters asked why she was striking. Her intelligent and **blunt** explanations of her school strike and reasons to fight climate change energized others to learn more and protest. Greta became an expert on environmental issues. She states scientific details regarding climate change and how climate change negatively affects animals, plants, and human society. People with Asperger's syndrome tend to **focus** intensely on topics that interest them. Greta considers her medical condition as a superpower.

Millions of people who learned about Greta through social and other media began to think of her as the representative of youth fighting to protect the planet. By the end of 2018, tens of thousands of students worldwide were striking for the climate.

Many young people believe that we are in a time of extreme crisis and that

1
2
3
4
5
6
7
8
9
10
11
12
13
14
15
16
17
18
19
20
21
22
23
24
25
26
27
28
29
30
31
32

immediate action is necessary, but most adults are not doing enough to reduce 33
our carbon footprint. On September 20, 2019, around 4,000,000 people joined a 34
worldwide demonstration that Greta inspired to protect Earth from climate change. 35

Also, in early 2019, when she was just 16, Greta received the first of three 36
nominations for the Nobel Peace Prize. The Norwegian politician who **nominated** 37
her told a newspaper reporter, "Greta Thunberg has launched a mass movement 38
which I see as a major contribution to peace." In December of 2019, *Time*, one of 39
the most influential magazines worldwide, chose Greta as "Person of the Year." This 40
award is given to one person who greatly influenced the world. Greta is also credited 41
with popularizing the phrase "climate strike," which Collins Dictionary named "Word 42
of the Year" in November of 2019. 43

Leaders of the United Nations and other international organizations asked Greta 44
to give speeches. As a result, she met many of the world's most powerful politicians. 45
She bluntly told them they are failing in their duty to protect the environment, their 46
inaction is destroying young people's futures, and they are irresponsible. 47

The "Gulbenkian Prize for Humanity" is an award given to someone who has 48
made great efforts to reduce climate change. The prize comes with 1,000,000 Euros. 49
Greta won the award in late 2019 and decided to donate the money to environmental 50
protection organizations. 51

Despite some mean criticism from others, including a few world leaders, such 52
as ex-president Donald Trump, Greta feels happy to be an environmental activist. 53
Millions of young people worldwide taking action to save the planet give her hope. 54
She wants everyone to protect our world now. 55

Greta at a large-scale climate
strike march in Berlin, Germany
on September 24, 2021

A What would be the best title for the passage?

    a. A Popular Teenager

    b. Problems Caused by Climate Change

    c. A Powerful Climate Activist

    d. Environmental Activists Around the World

B Write numbers to show the order of the events.

    _1_   Greta was born in Stockholm, Sweden.

    _____   She became depressed for several years.

    _____   *Time* chose her as "Person of the Year."

    _____   People began to think of her as the leader of young environmentalists.

    _____   She started protesting against climate change by herself.

    _____   The phrase "climate strike" was named "Word of the Year."

    _7_   She won a lot of money and donated it to protect the environment.

C Circle "C" for the correct information and "I" for the incorrect information. If the information is incorrect, revise the sentence.

> **Ex.** Greta decided to stop going to school on Fridays at the age of eight.
>
>   [C /(I)]   *Greta decided to stop going to school on Fridays at the age of 15.*

1. Greta thinks of her medical condition as a problem.

    [C / I]   _____

2. Around 4,000,000 people joined a European demonstration she inspired in 2019.

    [C / I]   _____

3. Greta kept the money she received with the "Gulbenkian Prize for Humanity."

    [C / I]   _____

4. When she was 18, Greta received her first nomination for a Noble Prize.

    [C / I]   _____

5. Greta bluntly spoke to the world's most powerful politicians.

[C / I] _____

6. Greta feels happy being an environmental activist.

[C / I] _____

Listening

A Listen to the questions while scanning the passage and circle the best answers.

B 04-07

1. **a.** depressed **b.** focused **c.** energized **d.** cheerful

2. **a.** cake **b.** airplane food **c.** oily dishes **d.** meat

3. **a.** a leaflet **b.** a notebook **c.** a sign **d.** a microphone

4. **a.** one million **b.** four million **c.** five million **d.** fifteen million

B Listen to the story and complete the script below.

B 08

Ways to Reduce Climate Change

All of us can take action to _____ climate change. Two simple actions are _____ and riding bicycles more often. _____ and reusing products are also helpful. When shopping, we _____ try to purchase food and goods _____ or manufactured locally. Using less energy in our _____, schools, and workplaces would help.

As some _____ activists say, "There is no _____ B." Do we want to give _____ children a healthy _____? If we want to do that, we should take action to _____ our Earth. For our children to have a good future, _____ action today is important.

Extinction Rebellion protesters in a climate change demonstration outside Buckingham Palace in London on September 3, 2020

Your Own Ideas

A Match the questions with the answers.

1. What is the most critical issue that your country must work to solve? ____

2. Would you join a demonstration to protect the environment? ____

3. How are you different from Greta? How are you similar? ____

4. Why are so many people not taking action to protect Earth? ____

5. If you won 100,000,000 yen, how would you use the money? ____

6. What are your sources of information about climate change? ____

a. She is focused, but I'm not. We are similar in that we worry about the future.

b. The most important issue to solve in my country is the problem of food waste.

c. I would buy a house for my parents, donate half the money to environmental organizations, and put the rest in the bank.

d. I would join a demonstration if I felt that the demonstration was safe.

e. Most of the information that I get about climate change comes from the internet and TV news shows.

f. Maybe they don't believe that Earth is in a state of crisis, or they don't know what to do.

B Work in pairs. Take turns asking the questions above and answering with your own ideas.

Critical Thinking

A Read each statement below and write your opinion using one of the five key phrases in the example.

B
09

Ex. If millions of young Japanese demonstrated against climate change, Japanese politicians would do more to protect our planet.

- **I strongly agree.** If that happened, politicians would definitely protect Earth.
- **I somewhat agree.** Some politicians with children will think about protecting the world for their kids, but a few politicians just want power and money.
- **I'm not sure.** I can't understand the thinking of politicians and their actions.
- **I somewhat disagree.** A minority of politicians will care about the opinions of young Japanese, but most Japanese have negative opinions of protests.
- **I strongly disagree.** Politicians work for senior citizens who contribute votes and money to their elections. They don't care about young people's opinions.

1. Energy conservation is the best way to save the planet.

   _____

2. Students should never skip classes to join demonstrations.

   _____

3. Choosing environmentalists to be political leaders will reduce climate change.

   _____

B Share your opinions with your classmates.

Taking Action

▶ Follow the steps to take action.

Step 1 ⟩ Research 10 ways to be more eco-friendly. Rank them in order of the most effortless action to the most difficult.

Step 2 ⟩ In a small group, share your ideas and encourage each other to do them for one week.

Step 3 ⟩ In class, report on the actions you did and those you did not.

Unit 9

Hair Donation

Supporters of Bald Children

Getting Ready

▶ Work in pairs. Look at the pictures and discuss the questions below.

1. What could be an explanation for why the child doesn't have hair?

2. If you lost your hair, what would you do?

3. What would you do to support sick friends?

4. Why is playing with friends so important for sick children?

Vocabulary

A Read the sentences and guess the meanings of the bold words.

1. The medicine caused her hair to fall out. Within two weeks, she was **bald**.

2. I know I did nothing wrong, but I felt terrible when rude people made **hurtful** comments after I lost my hair.

3. People who are different from others often have **social challenges**, for example, making friends and being treated fairly.

4. I don't want to grow a mustache or a beard, so I **shave** my face every morning.

5. A simple way to show **solidarity** with others is to share or like their social media posts.

6. The doctor is giving my father powerful medicines to kill cancer. I hope this **chemotherapy** will save his life.

7. Because of **discrimination**, African Americans could not eat in the same restaurants or go to the same hospitals as European Americans in some states.

B Fill in the blanks with the bold words above. Change the form if necessary.

Ex. LGBTQ people around the world are suffering from many types of _discrimination_.

1. The _____ made me lose hair and feel sick, but it saved my life.

2. Adults, who have more life experience and self-confidence than children, are usually better at dealing with _____.

3. The barber was scared to _____ customers' faces when he was an assistant.

4. We showed _____ with the sick children by sending games and toys.

5. My parents told me never to say _____ things to other people, but when I got angry, I often made rude jokes to make my enemies feel bad.

6. Most boys do not want to lose their hair, but when many boys become middle-aged men, they start to lose hair and go _____.

Reading

▶ Read the passage. Then, answer the following questions.

B
11

Four-year-old Teeba from Iraq, five-year-old Eden from the UK, and eleven-year-old Sam from the US are three among thousands of children who lose their hair every year.

Injuries, diseases, and even treatments to cure illnesses are why children become **bald** or almost bald. Some children lose their hair because of diseases they are born with or illnesses that develop as they grow up. Some medicines, especially those used to fight cancer, unintentionally bring about hair loss. Victims of fires may not be able to regrow hair on burned skin.

Fighting against injuries and diseases takes tremendous physical strength. On top of that, a significant change in appearance adds emotional stress. People often stare at bald children. Some make rude comments or **hurtful** jokes. At times, other children are afraid of them. As a result, many hairless children struggle with both medical conditions and **social challenges**. It is a lot to handle.

Thankfully, volunteers around the world are stepping up to help these children. For example, after an elementary school child in the US state of Colorado lost her hair because of cancer treatment, a friend **shaved** her own head. The friend wanted to show the sick girl that she was not alone. Soon afterward, 80 students, five teachers, and another friend's mother gathered in the school's gymnasium. They shaved their heads to show **solidarity** and raise money to help children fighting cancer.

Wigs made from human hair bring comfort to many bald children. High-quality wigs look like natural hair.

Every year in Changchun, China, around 20 women gather in a beauty salon to cut their long hair. Most of them prepare by not cutting their hair for years. Chinese wigmakers ask for hair donations to be 40 centimeters or longer. Children at a nearby cancer hospital receive the wigs.

The father of one child being treated at the cancer hospital said that his daughter had been taking **chemotherapy** for several months. She stopped wanting to play outside because other children mistreated her. However, her attitude improved after she wore a wig. One of the hospital's nurses said that wigs help protect children from social **discrimination**.

In Japan, the Japan Hair Donation & Charity (JHD&C) helps children receive free

1
2
3
4
5
6
7
8
9
10
11
12
13
14
15
16
17
18
19
20
21
22
23
24
25
26
27
28
29
30
31
32

An eight-year-old boy got his head shaved at the "Saving by Shaving" event at Boston Children's Hospital on April 3, 2019.

wigs. Kiichi Watanabe, the hairstylist who founded JHD&C, said in a Kyodo News article that one of his customers stopped visiting after she became bald. So wanting to help people like her, he founded the NPO to encourage people to donate cut hair, collect hair from beauty salons, produce wigs, and donate those wigs.

Human hair wigs cost around 300,000 yen, which many people cannot afford. JHD&C has given away over 400 wigs so far. Almost 500 people are waiting for high-quality realistic wigs. One high school student said that she had not smiled for a long time. She finally smiled after wearing the wig she had received and looking at herself in a mirror.

A girl in the UK who lost her hair when she became sick at the age of eight said that losing her hair caused her great sadness. Her hair, she said, had been her best characteristic. Wearing a wig that looked like her natural hair improved her mental health. She survived her illness. Now a teenager, she grows her hair long, and she regularly cuts and donates it to help younger children.

Donating hair is something that many people could do. The average human-hair wig requires around 20 ponytails. More people need wigs than wigs are available. Imagine how many children could be helped if more ordinary people, like us, donated some hair, money, or time to organizations like JHD&C. Children are waiting for assistance.

33
34
35
36
37
38
39
40
41
42
43
44
45
46
47
48
49
50
51
52
53
54

Elementary school students in California had their heads shaved at a charity event. They raised over 30,000 dollars for children fighting cancer.

A What would be the best title for the passage?

    a. Diseases that Cause Children to Lose Hair

    b. Helping and Understanding Children with Hair Loss

    c. Helping Sick Children to Grow Hair Again

    d. Wigmakers for Young Children

B Write numbers to show the order of the events.

    _1_   A doctor tells a child that he/she is sick.

    _____   He/She starts to feel better and smiles more often.

    _____   Because of some rude children, he/she loses confidence and feels sad.

    _____   The doctor gives medicine to him/her.

    _____   The medical treatment causes him/her to lose hair.

    _____   He/She receives a wig and wears it.

    _7_   He/She gets better and donates his/her long natural hair to others.

C Circle "C" for the correct information and "I" for the incorrect information. If the information is incorrect, revise the sentence.

    Ex. Treatments to cure illnesses are reasons why children become hairy.

        [C /(I)]   _Treatments to cure illnesses are reasons why children become bald._

    1. Fighting against injuries and diseases takes a small amount of physical strength.

        [C / I]   _____

    2. Many hairless children struggle with both medical conditions and social challenges.

        [C / I]   _____

    3. Unfortunately, volunteers around the world are stepping up to help sick children.

        [C / I]   _____

    4. A friend of a sick child shaved her face to show solidarity.

        [C / I]   _____

5. The Japan Hair Donation & Charity provides free wigs to sick children.

[C / I] _____

6. Donating hair is something that only a few people can do.

[C / I] _____

Listening

A Listen to the questions while scanning the passage and circle the best answers.

B
12-15

1. **a.** dozens   **b.** hundreds   **c.** thousands   **d.** millions

2. **a.** hurtful   **b.** funny   **c.** intelligent   **d.** angry

3. **a.** fake   **b.** fashionable   **c.** unstylish   **d.** natural

4. **a.** loneliness   **b.** social distance   **c.** coldness   **d.** social discrimination

B Listen to the story and complete the script below.

B
16

Assistance for Children Losing Hair

Volunteers, including very young children, are _____ their hair and mailing the cut _____ to organizations that make _____ for needy children. Hair stylists are _____ their hair-cutting skills to help the _____. And wigmakers are donating their time to _____ the free wigs. In some places, _____ as in the school mentioned in the _____, students are showing solidarity with sick _____ by shaving their heads. This is true _____.

The Indian company that this man works for sells hair products and donates wigs to cancer patients in India.

Your Own Ideas

A Match the questions with the answers.

1. Would you shave your head to show support for a friend fighting cancer? ____

2. Why do some children say hurtful comments to others who look different? ____

3. If a friend started to lose hair, what would you say or do? ____

4. What are the good and bad points of wearing face masks? ____

5. How much time do you spend taking care of your hair every morning? ____

6. What are three things you do to stay healthy? ____

a. I would tell that friend I will always be by their side.

b. Some children are bullies, but often children speak without considering how others feel.

c. I eat nutritious food, exercise three times a week, and listen to music.

d. A good point is that they can stop the spread of diseases, but a bad point is that they are hot in summer.

e. Maybe not. That is too much for me, but I would try to help in other ways.

f. I spend around 10 minutes getting my hair ready before going out.

B Work in pairs. Take turns asking the questions above and answering with your own ideas.

Critical Thinking

A Read each statement below and write your opinion using one of the five key phrases in the example.

B
17

Ex. Schools should require everyone to donate their hair at least once.

- **I strongly agree.** If everyone donated hair, there would be enough wigs.
- **I somewhat agree.** That would provide a lot of hair, which is good, but some people might not have enough hair themselves.
- **I'm not sure.** I've never thought about this topic, so I can't decide now.
- **I somewhat disagree.** There would be benefits for many sick people, but donating hair should be a personal choice.
- **I strongly disagree.** The schools shouldn't be able to force students to change their personal appearance to that extent.

1. Most young people pay too much attention to appearance.

   _____

2. The government should provide free wigs to people who want them.

   _____

3. The buying and selling of body parts, like kidneys, lungs, etc., should be legal.

   _____

B Share your opinions with your classmates.

Taking Action

▶ Follow the steps to take action.

Step 1 ⟩ In a small group, brainstorm body parts, besides hair, that can be donated, and decide on one body part for each student to research.

Step 2 ⟩ Search for information about how donors get those parts and how many people need them. Prepare a poster for a presentation.

Step 3 ⟩ Give your presentation in front of classmates.

Homeless People

Joshua Coombes

Getting Ready

▶ Work in pairs. Look at the pictures and discuss the questions below.

1. Have you seen homeless people anywhere in Japan?

2. What are some of the needs of people who live like this?

3. How often do you get your hair cut, take a bath or shower, and change clothes?

4. What are actions that some people take to help the homeless?

Vocabulary

A Read the sentences and guess the meanings of the bold words.

1. Her college requires community service activities. Her volunteer work at a foodbank **inspired** her to find a job helping the poor after graduating.

2. On cold nights, a **critical** question homeless people with little money consider is whether to pay for a hotel room or sleep in a park and save their money.

3. City officials worry that tourists will be **bothered** by the sight of the homeless.

4. Newspaper articles about the homeless never made me care about them. But photographs **humanized** the issue. Now I know they are ordinary people.

5. Common **stereotypes** of the homeless are that they are alcoholics or mentally ill. These ideas are not correct for all the homeless.

6. Food **nourishes** our bodies, and love nourishes our souls. This is true for all.

7. The homeless exist in Japan, the US, and many countries around the **globe**.

B Fill in the blanks with the bold words above. Change the form if necessary.

> **Ex.** The meals that _nourish_ me the most physically and emotionally are the ones I enjoy with family and friends.

1. Mother Teresa _____ millions of people worldwide to help others.

2. Common _____ of Japanese people are that they are rich and fashionable, but these are not true for all Japanese.

3. The growing number of homeless people in the park _____ parents, so they do not let children go to the park alone anymore.

4. To attend college or not is a _____ decision that can affect young people's futures.

5. The book reminded me that the homeless old men had once been young people with dreams like mine. It _____ those men.

6. Most major cities around the _____ have rich and poor people.

Reading

▶ Read the passage. Then, answer the following questions.

B
19

Joshua Coombes, a young British man, is the founder of the movement 1
"DoSomethingForNothing." It is a concept that has **inspired** thousands of people 2
worldwide to help other people. 3

Before starting "DoSomethingForNothing," he had a background that would 4
not impress many people. In his own words, he was not a good student. He became 5
a punk rock guitarist and part-time bartender. Then, he switched to working as 6
a hairdresser. While doing that job, he developed the **critical** skills of sincerely 7
listening and speaking from the heart to others. 8

Every day, as he walked to and from work, he saw a lot of homeless people. Their 9
suffering **bothered** him, but there did not seem to be a way to help them. 10

One day, while on the way to a friend's house, Joshua stopped to speak with 11
a homeless man whom he often saw around town. He remembered that his 12
hairdressing tools were in his bag, and he offered the homeless man a free haircut. 13
They spent about an hour together in conversation, and the man was thrilled. Joshua 14
was also happy. He had learned the importance of making other people feel good. So, 15
he continued giving free haircuts and talking to homeless people around his city. 16

Afterward, with the permission of the homeless people, Joshua started uploading 17
before- and after-haircut photographs to an Instagram account that he decided to 18
name "DoSomethingForNothing." He also wrote simple explanations to help people 19
understand the photographs. 20

The purpose of uploading the photographs and stories is to **humanize** the issue 21
of homelessness, in other words, to remind people that the homeless are humans, 22
just like those of us with homes and jobs. In addition, Joshua wants to make people 23
smile, destroy **stereotypes**, and encourage others to take action to make the world 24
more humane. 25

His photographs and stories developed into a global movement. His Instagram 26
account has followers from almost every country in the world. Joshua became an 27
inspiration for thousands of people who want to make the world a better place, but 28
do not know what to do. 29

In an online video, Joshua also asks us a critical question: "What world do we 30
want to live in?" Then, he advises us to find what **nourishes** our hearts and take 31
action. We cannot change the **globe**, but we can make other people's lives happier. 32

For Joshua, the smile of a person who has received a haircut is nourishment. 33
One follower, a veterinarian, started volunteering to give medical aid to homeless 34
people's pets. A musician decided to play music with homeless people. And a doctor 35
treats homeless people for free. The list of people helping others around the globe 36
continues to grow. 37

Local and global NGOs contacted Joshua after his "DoSomethingForNothing" 38
Instagram account grew popular. Many organizations asked for advice and 39
invited him to visit. Some requested that he give speeches and train their staff and 40
volunteers. As a result, he gave up his job and now spends all his time taking action 41
to help other people without expecting anything in return. International news 42
organizations often report on his activities. 43

He recently wrote a book about his experiences. The title is, of course, *Do* 44
Something for Nothing. His book includes photographs from his Instagram account, 45
and it tells the stories of homeless people around the globe in more detail. It destroys 46
negative stereotypes, humanizes a worldwide issue, and teaches readers that they 47
can make a critical difference in the lives of others. 48

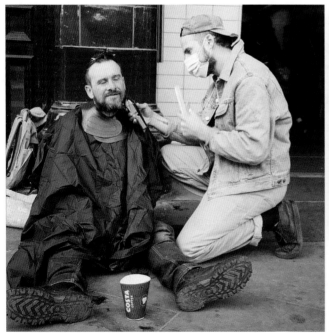

Left: Joshua offers free haircuts to the homeless on the streets of London. Right: "The Story of Us with Morgan Freeman," a documentary series on the National Geographic Channel, introduced Joshua.

A What would be the best title for the passage?

    a. Nourish Yourself by Helping Others

    b. Understanding Homelessness

    c. Jobs that Make the World Better

    d. Stereotypes of Homeless People

B Write numbers to show the order of the events.

    __1__   Joshua was a bad student.

    _____   He became a hairdresser.

    _____   He started giving free haircuts to the homeless.

    _____   He played in a band and worked as a bartender.

    _____   NPOs worldwide asked him for assistance.

    _____   His Instagram account became popular.

    __7__   He wrote a book about his experiences.

C Circle "C" for the correct information and "I" for the incorrect information. If the information is incorrect, revise the sentence.

    Ex. Joshua is a middle-aged British man.

        [C /Ⓘ]   *Joshua is a young British man.*

1. Two critical skills for Joshua are listening and speaking clearly.

    [C / I] _____

2. Joshua saw homeless people every day on the way to and from work.

    [C / I] _____

3. Joshua named his Instagram account "DoSomethingForNothing."

    [C / I] _____

4. Joshua became an inspiration for a few people.

    [C / I] _____

5. Joshua advises us to find what nourishes our hearts and take action.

[C / I] _____

6. Joshua's book tells the stories of homeless people in less detail.

[C / I] _____

Listening

A Listen to the questions while scanning the passage and circle the best answers.

B
20-23

1.   **a.** their suffering   **b.** their smell   **c.** their hairstyles   **d.** their looks

2.   **a.** nervous   **b.** scared   **c.** ashamed   **d.** thrilled

3.   **a.** permission   **b.** contracts   **c.** money   **d.** gifts

4.   **a.** society   **b.** critical thoughts   **c.** humanity   **d.** stereotypes

B Listen to the story and complete the script below.

B
24

From Being Helped to Helping Others

Mr. Sasaki had a difficult _____. He left his hometown and moved to Tokyo. His _____ was to be a writer, but he _____. Part-time jobs did not pay _____ for an apartment. After sleeping in internet cafés and _____ food from 100-yen shops, he became very _____. Luckily, he found Moyai, an NPO that _____ the homeless. Moyai helped him to _____ a place to stay and a _____. He regained his health. Today, he is _____ his experiences to help others in _____.

An organization similar to Moyai organized this Tokyo soup kitchen.

Your Own Ideas

A Match the questions with the answers.

1. What activities nourish your heart? ___

2. What have you recently done for free that helped someone else? ___

3. Would you feel comfortable talking with a homeless person? ___

4. Would you please describe a person who inspires you? ___

5. What is a critical skill that you want to improve? Why? ___

6. How is Joshua Coombes similar to and different from you? ___

a. No. I wouldn't know what I could talk about with a stranger.

b. Playing with pets and spending time with my friends nourish my heart.

c. He and I want to make the world better for others. He seems to enjoy talking with strangers, but I'm not comfortable doing that.

d. I've helped my brother with his homework. I also gave my train seat to an old person this morning.

e. My sister is making a living as an artist even though people told her it would be difficult. She inspires me to follow my dreams.

f. I want to improve my typing skills so I can finish my homework faster.

B Work in pairs. Take turns asking the questions above and answering with your own ideas.

Critical Thinking

A Read each statement below and write your opinion using one of the five key phrases in the example.

Ex. Each year, college students should be required to do community service activities, such as helping homeless people.

- **I strongly agree.** Helping others is a human duty, and we can learn about many critical issues through community service.
- **I somewhat agree.** Community service should be required of first- and second-year students, but not older students who need time for job hunting.
- **I'm not sure.** I've never thought about this, so I need time to think about it.
- **I somewhat disagree.** The activities should be encouraged, but not required.
- **I strongly disagree.** The only duty of students is studying. Also, many college students need to earn money for their living and education expenses.

---

1. Most homeless people are homeless because of the bad decisions they made.

_____

2. We can help the homeless to solve personal problems, find jobs, and get homes.

_____

3. The government should provide low-cost housing to the poor for three years.

_____

B Share your opinions with your classmates.

Taking Action

▶ Follow the steps to take action.

Step 1 Research Japanese organizations that help the homeless. Then, choose the one you believe does the most valuable work and write a short summary.

Step 2 In a small group, read your summaries and choose the one you want to help.

Step 3 Think of an action you can take to help the organization. You might collect money or goods and donate what you collect.

Cleaner Places

Nadia Sparkes

Getting Ready

▶ Work in pairs. Look at the pictures and discuss the questions below.

1. Have you seen any places covered with trash?

2. What do you know about animals that eat trash and then get injured or die?

3. Would you like to join activities like this one?

4. What are the most common types of trash that you see?

Vocabulary

A Read the sentences and guess the meanings of the bold words.

1. In my community, the correct way to **dispose** of paper is to leave it at the trash station on Tuesday.

2. Since she worries about the dangers of nuclear power plants, she supports the politicians with **anti**-nuclear power positions.

3. The bullies **insulted** the student by saying he was ugly and stupid.

4. Parents should scold their children when they do bad things and **praise** them when they do good things.

5. A group of **like-minded** people usually enjoy the same activity because they have similar ideas and interests.

6. After I dropped my empty bento box and tea bottle on the school floor, the principal told me to pick up my trash and never **litter** again.

7. The river is full of trash. I do not want to swim in that **filthy** water.

B Fill in the blanks with the bold words above. Change the form if necessary.

Ex. <u>Anti</u>-gun-control Americans believe that they have a right to keep and carry guns.

1. Sometimes, _____ others with rude words is just as cruel as physically hurting them.

2. My brother and I are not _____. He loves hip-hop while I like jazz.

3. I used to relax at this river, but now many people picnic and _____ plates, straws, and cans. I don't enjoy the river anymore.

4. Ten years ago, the beaches were clean, but now they are _____.

5. Correctly _____ of the plastic trash on Tuesday and the paper trash on Wednesday. If you make a mistake, the neighbors get angry.

6. Our teacher _____ us for helping to clean up the campus.

▶ Read the passage. Then, answer the following questions.

B
27

One simple action that we can all take to make our world better is picking up | 1
and properly **disposing** of trash. In 2019, the Prime Minister of the UK gave Nadia | 2
Sparkes an award for her **anti**-litter campaign. She was just 13 years old then. | 3

While many people today spend their days peering into phone and computer | 4
screens, Nadia works to beautify her community. When she started riding her bicycle | 5
to her high school, she saw many cigarette butts, plastic bottles, empty cans, and | 6
other trash. She was upset and thought something had to be done. So Nadia decided | 7
to pick up and properly dispose of trash every day. | 8

When she first arrived at school with a bike basket full of trash, rude students | 9
insulted Nadia instead of **praising** her. They said that she was weird and called her | 10
Trash Girl. Some people use the word "trash" to hurt others. | 11

Nadia received both abuse and praise while encouraging people everywhere | 12
to protect nature. Her anti-litter campaign is a clear example of the environmental | 13
movement's slogan "Think globally, act locally." | 14

Instead of feeling ashamed and embarrassed by that insulting nickname, she | 15
developed a Facebook page with her parents' help and named it Team Trash Girl. As | 16
a result, Nadia is now respected by many people worldwide. In their view, the words | 17
Trash Girl represents a person who cares about nature and her community. | 18

Thousands of **like-minded** people have joined the Team Trash Girl Facebook | 19
page. Many routinely pick up trash, share photographs of their activities, and post | 20
comments on the topic of trash. It is a community for like-minded people who are | 21
supporting each other and making the world a cleaner place. Former Prime Minister | 22
Theresa May was so impressed that she wrote a letter praising Nadia and gave her | 23
an award for her activities. | 24

Unfortunately, school bullies continued abusing Nadia. One day a student threw | 25
juice in her face. After that, another student hit her, and a student later threatened | 26
her with a knife. Her high school was not doing enough to support and protect her. | 27
Luckily, another high school with like-minded staff and students welcomed her with | 28
open arms. The new school actively supports her work to encourage people to stop | 29
littering and to pick up trash. | 30

You can view an inspiring YouTube video of Nadia riding a bicycle on the way to | 31
school and stopping to pick up trash. It is a simple activity that we can all do with | 32

our friends, family, club members, and classmates. 33

While you read these words in this passage, somewhere in the world, other 34 people are taking action to clean Earth. Scuba diving club members are gathering 35 trash from rivers, lakes, and ocean floors. Groups of hikers are enjoying hikes while 36 picking up trash. Truck drivers are stretching their bodies while bending down to 37 collect cans and plastic bags when taking breaks from driving. 38

The benefits of clean-up activities are obvious. You can change a **filthy** 39 environment into a beautiful one. Other benefits are less noticeable. By removing 40 trash, you are preventing the deaths of animals you cannot see. Millions of animals 41 die from eating plastic bags and other trash every year. Also, recycling used cans and 42 bottles requires less energy and produces less pollution than creating new cans and 43 bottles. Your work reduces climate change and other global problems. 44

People who pick up trash comment on how rewarding the experience feels. The 45 change in the local environment is obvious, and you can be proud of yourself. 46

Proud of her achievement, Nadia smiles at her mother.

A What would be the best title for the passage?

    a. Cleaning the Streets

    b. Heroes of the UK

    c. Trash Pickers Helping Earth

    d. High School Problems

B Write numbers to show the order of the events.

    _1_   Nadia became a high school student.

    _____   Rude students insulted her.

    _____   After the prime minister gave her an award, the bullying continued.

    _____   She started arriving at school with a bike basket full of trash.

    _____   Thousands of people joined the Team Trash Girl Facebook page.

    _____   She was upset by the amount of trash she saw on the way to school.

    _7_   She changed to a safer and more supportive high school.

C Circle "C" for the correct information and "I" for the incorrect information. If the information is incorrect, revise the sentence.

    Ex. Nadia is a citizen of the US.

        [C /Ⓘ]   _Nadia is a citizen of the UK._

    1. Nadia was driving a car when she went to high school.

        [C / I]   _____

    2. The word "trash" is often used to compliment people.

        [C / I]   _____

    3. Nadia was bullied by some high school students.

        [C / I]   _____

    4. There are like-minded staff and students in Nadia's new school.

        [C / I]   _____

5. The benefits of clean-up activities are not noticeable.

[C / I] _____

6. Thousands of animals around the world are killed by trash every year.

[C / I] _____

Listening

A Listen to the questions while scanning the passage and circle the best answers.

B
28-31

1.   **a.** anti-tax   **b.** anti-crime   **c.** anti-litter   **d.** anti-war

2.   **a.** her community   **b.** her room   **c.** her school   **d.** her neighbors' homes

3.   **a.** Instagram   **b.** Facebook   **c.** Twitter   **d.** YouTube

4.   **a.** productive   **b.** problematic   **c.** rewarded   **d.** energetic

B Listen to the story and complete the script below.

B
32

The Joys of Plogging

Eric speaking online to thousands of people about plogging

Plocka upp is Swedish for _____ up, and *jogga* means _____. Plogging, the English term, has been spreading worldwide since Erik Ahlström _____ the trend in 2016. He decided to _____ trash while running. Other runners _____ him. Ploggers believe that plogging is _____ than jogging

Eric carrying bags of trash after plogging on a small island in Sweden

because plogging involves more _____ and burns more calories. _____, their running routes _____ more attractive.

Your Own Ideas

A Match the questions with the answers. B 65

1. Why do some people leave their trash on beaches? ___

2. How can we safely pick up trash? ___

3. What would you do with your trash after a camping trip? ___

4. Have you ever littered? Tell the truth. ___

5. Where do you often see trash in your town? ___

6. What would you do if you saw someone littering? ___

a. I might politely suggest that the person use a trash can.

b. I often see trash on the sides of rivers and busy roads.

c. I would take my trash home and put it in trash cans.

d. I dropped snack packages on the ground when I was younger.

e. It should be safe if we wear gloves or use tools to pick up trash.

f. Maybe they are lazy, or they don't care about animals and other people.

B Work in pairs. Take turns asking the questions above and answering with your own ideas.

Critical Thinking

A Read each statement below and write your opinion using one of the five key phrases in the example.

Ex. People litter because they do not understand that trash severely damages the environment.

- **I strongly agree.** People who litter know nothing about environmental issues.
- **I somewhat agree.** Many people who litter don't pay attention to environmental news, but the trash problem is obvious.
- **I'm not sure.** I have no idea why people litter.
- **I somewhat disagree.** Everyone knows that littering negatively affects nature, but maybe they don't know the seriousness of the problem.
- **I strongly disagree.** The mass media constantly reports on litter and other environmental problems. People who litter just do not care about nature.

---

1. Plogging should be a required gym-class activity for college students.

2. Littering should be legally punished by a fine of more than 100,000 yen.

3. We should send radioactive waste to the moon.

B Share your opinions with your classmates.

Taking Action

▶ Follow the steps to take action.

Step 1 In a small group, decide the location, date, and time for a clean-up activity. Brainstorm the items you will need (e.g. gloves and bags).

Step 2 Join your fellow students at the meeting location and photograph the location before and after the clean-up.

Step 3 In class, report what you have done. Also, you might share your pictures on an SNS page to encourage others to plan similar events.

Artworks

Chris Jordan

Getting Ready

▶ Work in pairs. Look at the pictures and discuss the questions below.

1. Why did a photographer decide to take this picture of a chained elephant leg?

2. What did the artist who created this statue want viewers to think about?

3. What strong message do you get from this huge wall painting?

4. If you could create art about a social problem, which topic would you choose?

Vocabulary

A Read the sentences and guess the meanings of the bold words.

B
34

1. Making the video about homeless people was a **transformative** experience. It changed how I view the issues of the homeless and my idea of success.

2. Photography and graphic designing are two popular careers in the art **field**.

3. Paintings, sculptures, movies, books, manga, music, poetry, and TikTok content that make people think or feel are types of **artworks**.

4. The media used charts and graphs to illustrate the **magnitude** of the worldwide suffering caused by COVID-19.

5. **Mass** consumption involves the factory production of millions of items for sale to people who think owning many goods equals happiness.

6. In **throwaway** societies, people quickly buy and throw objects away.

7. Your presentations should include **statistics** such as what percent of artists make a living by selling their art, average prices for their paintings, etc.

B Fill in the blanks with the bold words above. Change the form if necessary.

B
66

Ex. Picasso's _artworks_ are about a variety of topics. His famous oil painting titled *Guernica* has an anti-war message.

1. Plastic pollution is of such _____ that it affects everyone on Earth.

2. The garbage problem is connected to the _____ production of goods.

3. Both of my parents work in the education _____. My dad is a college teacher and my mom is a high school principal.

4. Journalists should use correct _____ when reporting the news.

5. On average, Americans dispose of almost two kilograms of garbage each day. The US is a clear example of a _____ culture.

6. My brother's history class was _____. He changed his major from sports science to history.

▶ Read the passage. Then, answer the following questions.

🎧 B 35

Creating works of beauty is the goal of some artists. Others create stylish, [1]
valuable items. **Transformative** artists are those in the art **field** who attempt to [2]
create **artworks** that change behavior. Artists worldwide are creating artworks to [3]
take action against sexual discrimination, nuclear war, animal abuse, pollution, and [4]
other global problems. [5]

Chris Jordan is a speaker, a photographer, and a filmmaker. His art is famous [6]
for its power to make people feel and think. People worldwide have seen his [7]
photographs, watched his videos, read his interviews, and listened to his talks. [8]

Some of his artworks deal with the **magnitude** of **mass** consumption and our [9]
throwaway society. His photograph of a baby albatross that died from eating [10]
plastic garbage is an excellent example. This image touched the hearts of millions. [11]
Afterward, some of them littered less or picked up trash. Such moving artworks are [12]
often more inspirational than **statistics**. [13]

As a child, Chris loved photography, but he did not believe enough in his skills. [14]
Instead, he studied law in college. Then, he worked in a law office. [15]

But he spent much of his free time wandering through the city of Seattle, [16]
Washington, with a camera. Finally, after a decade of unhappily working in the law [17]
field, he became a professional photographer. [18]

In 2005, Chris self-published a collection of photographs titled *Intolerable Beauty*. [19]
The collection includes beautiful images of millions of cell phones, car parts, cans, [20]
and other things that are disposed of on a daily basis. [21]

In two continuing collections of artworks, titled *Running the Numbers: An* [22]
American Self-Portrait and *Running the Numbers II: Portraits of global mass culture*, [23]
Chris combines statistics with photographs of social and global problems to express [24]
powerful messages. [25]

For example, Chris took photographs of 2.4 million pieces of plastic garbage from [26]
the ocean and used his computer to create art. The artwork resembles Hokusai's [27]
famous print *Under the Wave off Kanagawa*. The 2.4 million pieces represent the [28]
estimated number of plastic pieces of garbage entering the ocean each hour. [29]

Another example is a forest image he created by using photographs of the [30]
remains of 139,000 cigarettes. Why 139,000? That statistic represents the cigarettes [31]
American people smoke and throw away every 15 seconds. [32]

Despite focusing on global problems, Chris believes there is hope. In 2010, he created a computer-generated image of a bridge using the names of one million NPOs that work to make the world a better place. The title is *E Pluribus Unum*, Latin for "one from many." It reminds us there are many groups and we can join together to improve our only world.

In 2011, Chris traveled to a remote part of Kenya. With the cooperation of NGOs saving wildlife, he took photographs of tribespeople, animals, homes, landscapes, and more. His photographs show the problem of poaching and how people are trying to live sustainably in Kenya.

On the internet, you can view for free the documentary he created in 2017 about ocean pollution and birdlife. It might transform your thinking about the magnitude of mass consumption and throwaway plastic goods.

After Chris completed his documentary about ocean pollution, he started a new art project to show the environmental problems caused by mining for materials to make batteries for electric cars and other electric products.

Within the wide field of art, millions of songwriters, painters, photographers, poets, storytellers, manga artists, and others are taking action to improve our lives. Around the world, many artists and other people are trying to save our planet. Shall we join them?

A powerful image from Chris Jordan's *Midway: Message from the Gyre*.

A What would be the best title for the passage?

    a. Transforming Garbage into Art

    b. Creating Artworks about Global Issues

    c. The Story of Great Photography

    d. Some Popular Artworks

B Write numbers to show the order of the events.

    _1_   Chris Jordan was a child who loved photography.

    _____   He studied law in college.

    _____   He finished a documentary that we can see for free online.

    _____   He published his own book about social problems in 2005.

    _____   In Kenya, he took photographs about poaching and sustainability.

    _____   He quit his job in the law firm to be a professional photographer.

    _7_   He worked on an art project related to mining.

C Circle "C" for the correct information and "I" for the incorrect information. If the information is incorrect, revise the sentence.

> **Ex.** Chris is a speaker, a photographer, and a musician.
>
> [C /(I)]   _Chris is a speaker, a photographer, and a filmmaker._

1. Artists in a few countries are taking action against various global problems.

    [C / I]   _____

2. Some of Chris' artworks deal with the magnitude of mass consumption and our throwaway society.

    [C / I]   _____

3. An estimated 2.4 million pieces of plastic garbage enter the ocean every day.

    [C / I]   _____

4. Photographs of the remains of 139,000 chopsticks were used for a forest image.

    [C / I]   _____

5. The artwork *E Pluribus Unum* includes the names of one million NPOs.

[C / I] _____

6. We can view the documentary about ocean pollution and birdlife on the internet.

[C / I] _____

Listening

A Listen to the questions while scanning the passage and circle the best answers.

1. **a.** traditional **b.** stylish **c.** modern **d.** transformative

2. **a.** write songs **b.** make videos **c.** take photographs **d.** give speeches

3. **a.** insects **b.** whales **c.** birds **d.** mammals

4. **a.** a forest **b.** an ocean **c.** a bridge **d.** the globe

B Listen to the story and complete the script below.

Great Female Indian Artist

Shweta Bhattad is an Indian artist _____ uses artworks to promote women's _____, girls' safety, and farmers' rights. One of her projects is collaborating with _____ to decorate _____. They make the calendars using waste paper, cloth, and organically _____ cotton. Each month tells the story _____ significant issues in the lives of local female farmers. And _____ calendar page contains _____. At the end of each month, that month's _____ page can be planted. Sales _____ go to the women who made the calendars.

Shweta is an activist artist in Nagpur, India.

Sprouts are growing from a calendar page.

Your Own Ideas

A Match the questions with the answers.

 B 67

1. If you could be a professional artist, what type of artist would you like to be? _____

2. Have you seen or listened to any artworks that express social problems? _____

3. If you were a rich and famous artist, how could you help the world? _____

4. Do you think art is important? Why or why not? _____

5. What do you know about people using art for health care? _____

6. What are your favorite types of art to see or listen to? _____

a. I'd like to be a professional animator.

b. My favorite types of art are photography and pottery.

c. I could sell my artworks and donate the money to help the homeless.

d. Art is important for several reasons. It helps us to see beauty, understand new perspectives, and become more creative.

e. Some college teachers teach art therapy. They say creating art makes people feel better.

f. I've seen illustrations about animal rights on some Facebook pages, and I've listened to many anti-war songs recently.

B Work in pairs. Take turns asking the questions above and answering with your own ideas.

Critical Thinking

A Read each statement below and write your opinion using one of the five key phrases in the example.

B
41

> Ex. All students from elementary school through college should take art classes.
>
> - **I strongly agree.** Art benefits students mentally, emotionally, and physically.
> - **I somewhat agree.** Art classes should be required from elementary to high school, but optional in college.
> - **I'm not sure.** The positive and negative points seem equal to me.
> - **I somewhat disagree.** Studying art has benefits for many students, but some students are not interested in art. Some won't need art in their future lives.
> - **I strongly disagree.** Art is less important than many other subjects, and the ability to create art is not necessary for life.

1. Children shouldn't see any artwork showing nude people.

   _____

2. All cities should provide free art classes and admission to art museums.

   _____

3. Shocking art expressing social issues is more important than beautiful art.

   _____

B Share your opinions with your classmates.

Taking Action

▶ Follow the steps to take action.

Step 1 Choose one significant issue and express it through any type of art (a photo collage, drawings, paintings, sculpture, dance, etc.).

Step 2 Study the issue enough for you to create an artwork that will make people think about the issue.

Step 3 In small groups, share your artwork with others. Give positive feedback.

Unit 13
Suicide Prevention

Kevin Hines

Getting Ready

▶ Work in pairs. Look at the pictures and discuss the questions below.

1. Does everyone who needs help with personal problems ask for help?

2. Is this kind of signboard helpful for depressed people?

3. When was the last time you helped a stranger? What happened?

4. What would you do if your friend looked depressed?

Vocabulary

A Read the sentences and guess the meanings of the bold words.

1. People suffering from **depression** have to fight against a deep sadness that lasts for a long time.

2. Rather than live in pain for years, some very sick people commit **suicide**.

3. After my grandmother died, I **regretted** that I had not given her more attention.

4. The man's **paranoia** was so strong that he could not believe anyone. He was constantly imagining that others were going to hurt him.

5. Some drug addicts and mentally ill people have **hallucinations**. They hear, see, feel, or smell things that are not real.

6. My brother cannot participate in active sports because of a heart **disorder**. His heart is weak.

7. Speaking in public is not easy, and I worry that people do not like me. Sometimes, just getting out of bed and going to school is a personal **struggle**.

B Fill in the blanks with the bold words above. Change the form if necessary.

> **Ex.** His parents abused him. He used alcohol to feel better. Counselors helped him overcome his _struggles_ with alcohol and trusting others.

1. People suffering from _____ do not easily trust others.

2. She said she _____ not asking for help because counseling could have helped her to solve her problems faster.

3. _____ counselors work to stop people from killing themselves.

4. He was in a deep _____ after his son died in a car accident.

5. Because of a rare blood _____, she needs to visit the hospital for medical care every month.

6. The mental patient suffers from _____. He sometimes speaks to people and plays with animals that do not exist.

▶ Read the passage. Then, answer the following questions.

🎧 B / 43

Kevin Hines has saved the lives of thousands of people suffering from **depression**. He is both a **suicide** prevention counselor and public speaker, and he is also a survivor of his own suicide attempt. At the age of 19, he jumped headfirst from San Francisco's Golden Gate Bridge. Kevin fell 68.5 meters into the Pacific Ocean.

It was an action that he instantly **regretted**. Turning his body around, he landed feet first. The impact broke bones in his lower back and one foot. Only 36 out of approximately 2,000 people who leaped from that bridge survived. Many of those survivors reported regretting jumping as soon as they started to fall.

Kevin has been struggling with depression, **paranoia**, and **hallucinations** since he was a teenager. When Kevin was 10, doctors gave him medication for a brain **disorder**. When that problem ended in his mid-teens, he discontinued that medication. Then, he soon started feeling the effects of bipolar disorder. This medical condition makes people swing from feeling extreme excitement and happiness to a deep, dark depression. In the following years, his parents separated, and he also broke up with his girlfriend.

Kevin repeatedly thought about ending his life, and he started writing and rewriting suicide notes. One day, he took a bus to the Golden Gate Bridge. As Kevin walked along the bridge, tears were pouring down his face, but no one stopped to ask if Kevin was OK or needed help. If someone had shown concern for him, he might not have jumped. No one did. He heard voices in his head telling him to jump.

Rescue workers pulled him from the water and rushed him to a hospital for emergency medical care. Then, he went to a mental hospital for help with his mental **struggles**.

Soon afterward, Kevin decided to share with the world his secret struggles with mental illness. Kevin wanted to give hope to other people who also lived with great pain. So, he told his story to students at a junior high school. In response, some of those students wrote letters to Kevin. Their messages were that his story motivated them to find help for their private struggles. This meaningful experience became the beginning of his career as a suicide prevention counselor.

Since then, he has spoken to thousands of students at high schools and colleges, and he has told his story on numerous TV talk shows and news shows. Kevin also started an organization to share information about mental health issues and suicide

1
2
3
4
5
6
7
8
9
10
11
12
13
14
15
16
17
18
19
20
21
22
23
24
25
26
27
28
29
30
31
32

prevention with people worldwide. In addition, he has co-written books on those 33
topics. And the documentary movie *Suicide: The Ripple Effect*, which he made 34
about his struggles and suicide attempt, has won international awards. But most 35
importantly, for Kevin, his movie saves lives. 36

Although decades have passed since his suicide attempt, he still struggles with 37
mental problems. But he has found ways to stay safe. When unhealthy thoughts 38
and behaviors return, he takes medication, speaks with counselors, exercises, eats 39
healthy food, meditates, and uses music therapy to keep mentally stable. 40

Kevin believes that being honest with one's pain is a step forward. Both thinking 41
about suicide and asking for help are nothing to be ashamed about. Today, he 42
reminds us that we should always offer our help to anyone who seems to be 43
suffering. We never know when kindness might save someone's life. 44

Kevin, a survivor from a jump off the Golden Gate Bridge, has been helping many depressed people.
https://www.instagram.com/kevinhinesstory/
http://www.KevinHinesStory.com

A What would be the best title for the passage?

    a. Staying Healthy in Stressful Times

    b. Mental Health Explained

    c. A Survivor Helping Others

    d. The Bridge in San Francisco

B Write numbers to show the order of the events.

    __1__   Kevin started taking medication at 10 years old.

    _____   No one asked if he was OK or not.

    _____   Students wrote that his speech helped them with their troubles.

    _____   He went to the Golden Gate Bridge.

    _____   He wrote books and made a documentary.

    _____   Voices told him to jump.

    __7__   He still has mental problems, but he works to help struggling people.

C Circle "C" for the correct information and "I" for the incorrect information. If the information is incorrect, revise the sentence.

> **Ex.** Bipolar disorder is a physical problem.
>
>   [C /(I)]   _Bipolar disorder is a mental problem._

1. He jumped off San Francisco's Golden Gate Building.

    [C / I]   _____

2. After his suicide attempt, Kevin spoke at a junior high school.

    [C / I]   _____

3. Kevin has shared his story on TV talk shows and news shows.

    [C / I]   _____

4. Kevin's organization helps people around North America.

    [C / I]   _____

5. Kevin has found ways to stay safe from unhealthy thoughts and behaviors.

[C / I] _____

6. Kevin also believes that asking for help is something to be ashamed of.

[C / I] _____

Listening

A Listen to the questions while scanning the passage and circle the best answers.

B 44-47

1.   **a.** excitement   **b.** depression   **c.** regret   **d.** satisfaction
2.   **a.** hand   **b.** back   **c.** head   **d.** rib
3.   **a.** medication   **b.** notes   **c.** letters   **d.** hope
4.   **a.** our dreams   **b.** our pain   **c.** our regrets   **d.** our medications

B Listen to the story and complete the script below.

B 48

Neighbors Saving Lives

The Australian government gave _____ of the Year Awards to Don _____ Moya Ritchie. The couple lived close to a _____ cliff where numerous people go to _____ suicide every year. When the Ritchies _____ anyone who appeared to be considering _____ off the cliff, they walked over, _____, and invited them to their house _____ tea. They saved almost 200 people _____ way. Kindness and smiles have the _____ to save lives. We should all be _____ to others.

This ocean cliff at the entrance to Sydney Harbor is a well-known location for committing suicide.

A Match the questions with the answers.

 B 69

1. What do you do to maintain your mental health?

___

2. What do you think about working as a suicide prevention counselor?

___

3. Why do some people feel depressed more often than other people?

___

4. If you saw someone crying in the street, what would you do?

___

5. Where can students with mental struggles find help at our school?

___

6. Have you ever regretted doing anything? What was it?

___

a. I watch movies, take hot baths, and eat out with my friends.

b. I regret that I was staring at my phone while walking. Unfortunately, I walked into an old lady. She fell down. I felt terrible.

c. Maybe they are dealing with terrible problems in their lives, or they suffer from mental or physical disorders.

d. I might ask if the person needed help. Otherwise, I would try to find a police officer to deal with the situation.

e. Students can talk to the school counselor or nurse or call a helpline.

f. It's a great job, but it's too much responsibility for me.

B Work in pairs. Take turns asking the questions above and answering with your own ideas.

Critical Thinking

A Read each statement below and write your opinion using one of the five key phrases in the example.

B
49

Ex. Social media makes young people communicate less with people around them.

- **I strongly agree.** Nowadays, most people stare at their phones instead of communicating with people around them. They care more about social media friends.
- **I somewhat agree.** Young people today do speak less to strangers but they also share the things they see or read on social media with nearby people.
- **I'm not sure.** I grew up with social media, so I don't know what life was like before it.
- **I somewhat disagree.** Verbal communication has declined, but my friends use social media to send messages to both people in other locations and those nearby.
- **I strongly disagree.** Social media brings people with the same interests together. It helps us find like-minded people in our communities.

1. All bridges should be completely fenced in order to prevent suicide.

2. Suicide for people with severe illnesses that cannot be healed should be legal.

3. All students should be required to study suicide and suicide prevention.

B Share your opinions with your classmates.

Taking Action

▶ Follow the steps to take action.

Step 1 ⟩ Research mental health and suicide prevention websites. Then, summarize essential points about these topics.

Step 2 ⟩ In a small group, share your results from the research and create a bilingual poster.

Step 3 ⟩ Hang your posters in appropriate locations.

Unit 14
Peacebuilding

Leymah Gbowee

Getting Ready

▶ **Work in pairs. Look at the pictures and discuss the questions below.**

1. Do you know what Martin Luther King Jr. did?

2. What do you know about Mahatma Gandhi?

3. What would you do if war was destroying your city?

4. Would you join a peaceful anti-war protest even if you might be arrested?

Vocabulary

A Read the sentences and guess the meanings of the bold words.

1. Martin Luther King Jr. and Mahatma Gandhi are perhaps two of the last century's most famous **peacebuilders**. Both died while trying to build peace.

2. The purpose of the skills-building workshops is to **empower** poor, undereducated youth so they can succeed and do great things with their lives.

3. The nuclear accident caused many **displaced** families. They had to leave their land and homes for years.

4. She lost family, friends, and money due to the war. Her future seemed **hopeless**.

5. She traveled for 10 hours to join the protest. Then, she gave speeches and marched 10 kilometers. She was so **exhausted** that she slept on the bus back.

6. In the US, the most common **faith** is Christianity, but in Iran, it is Islam.

7. The UN wants countries with serious disagreements to choose **nonviolent** ways, such as discussions, to solve their problems instead of turning to war.

B Fill in the blanks with the bold words above. Change the form if necessary.

Ex. My situation seemed *hopeless*, but my mom helped me to overcome my troubles.

1. The United Nations has many duties as a _____. Its most important aim is to end fighting.

2. I did not believe my life could get better, but I was _____ by counseling. I felt stronger and looked forward to taking action to improve my life.

3. Some demonstrations involve fighting, but others are _____.

4. There are various _____ around the world, for instance, Christianity, Buddhism, Islam, and Hinduism.

5. I was so _____ after work that I almost slept during dinner.

6. In March of 2022, millions of Ukrainians became _____ after Russia invaded.

▶ Read the passage. Then, answer the following questions.

Leymah speaks about "The Role of Women at the Front Lines of Peace Building" during a Visionary Women Salon at the Beverly Wilshire, A Four Seasons Hotel in California on May 5, 2015.

Leymah Gbowee told an interviewer, "Don't wait for a Gandhi, don't wait for a King, don't wait for a Mandela. You are your own Mandela, you are your own Gandhi, you are your own King."

Leymah, born in Liberia in 1972, rose from being a victim of violence to becoming an inspiring **peacebuilder**. She won the Nobel Peace Prize in 2011 for **empowering** women to end violence.

In 1989, Leymah celebrated her high school graduation, and war broke out in Liberia's countryside. Then, when she was a college student, war came to her city, Monrovia. She saw soldiers kill her neighbors. Leymah and some of her family escaped on a ship to Ghana, where she lived with 50,000 **displaced** Liberians in a crowded refugee camp.

After the fighting had decreased in 1991, she returned to Monrovia, discovering the air smelled of death, relatives had died, and bombs had destroyed many buildings. Monrovia lacked electricity, running water, or working toilets.

In Monrovia, Leymah married a man from the refugee camp. Her husband was abusive. He beat her. Meanwhile, soldiers continued fighting in the countryside, and in the following year, the war returned to Monrovia, but they survived even though life was scary and uncomfortable.

Hundreds of thousands of Liberians needed counseling for physical and mental trauma. Older soldiers had forced approximately 15,000 young children to become soldiers. Soldiers sexually abused thousands of helpless women. Leymah studied counseling and she counseled many people who felt **hopeless**.

In 1996, soldiers destroyed her home, so she escaped to Ghana with two children and her husband. In Ghana, she had another child, but her husband still beat her. 33

Later that year, she ran away from her husband and returned to her father's 34
home in Liberia. At 26, she was single with three children and pregnant again. 35
Leymah thought her life was hopeless. 36

However, she realized her children needed her to provide for them. So she 37
searched for employment and found an empowering job as a counselor for a church 38
organization. Her relatives cared for her children while she traveled across Liberia 39
to help others. She often felt **exhausted** from working so hard. 40

Then in 1999, the violence increased across Liberia. In 2002, Leymah organized 41
an international peacebuilding conference, where the Women in Peacebuilding 42
Network (WIPNET) was founded. Participants asked her to lead the Liberia section. 43

Leymah taught communication skills to other women. From morning until 44
night, she studied, counseled, and organized. Exhausted, she often slept at her 45
desk. A voice in a dream told her, "Gather women to pray for peace!" Then, she 46
organized gatherings where Christian and Muslim women prayed and sang together. 47
Historically, members of those **faiths** rarely cooperated in Liberia. 48

Leymah decided action was necessary, too. Using the radio, WIPNET invited 49
women to **nonviolent** public marches. At that time, marching was illegal and 50
dangerous. Sometimes soldiers killed protesters. However, thousands of mothers 51
gathered and marched to the capitol with signs demanding the end of violence. 52

Local and international media, soldiers, and politicians paid attention to the 53
women. Leymah spoke about peace and women's rights. Women of different faiths 54
sang, "We want peace, no more war." But, unfortunately, the violence lasted for many 55
more months. 56

Meanwhile, army leaders were meeting for luxurious meals and peace talks at 57
expensive hotels, as ordinary people were starving, being displaced, or dying from 58
gunshots. In July of 2003, angry women led by Leymah blocked the meeting room's 59
entrances. The women announced that they would not leave until the leaders 60
ended the war. Police threatened to arrest Leymah, but the women continued their 61
nonviolent protest. 62

Fourteen years of war ended the following month thanks to Leymah's 63
peacebuilding activities. After the war, Leymah continued working for women's 64
rights and peace in Africa. Winning the Nobel Peace Prize with two other women in 65
2011 brought more attention to her life and her nonviolent methods to bring about 66
social change. Young people worldwide facing severe challenges will, hopefully, gain 67
knowledge and strength from her words and actions. 68

A What would be the best title for the passage?

    a. Violence in Liberia

    b. Protesting for Mother's Rights

    c. Displaced Liberians

    d. A Woman Working for Peace

B Write numbers to show the order of the events.

    __1__   Leymah was born in Liberia.

    _____   Soldiers killed her neighbors in front of her.

    _____   While dreaming, a voice told her to gather women to pray for peace.

    _____   With other women, she started a peace group for women in Liberia.

    _____   She became a counselor.

    _____   She became displaced for the first time.

    __7__   Her peacebuilding actions ended the 14 years of war.

C Circle "C" for the correct information and "I" for the incorrect information. If the information is incorrect, revise the sentence.

    Ex. Leymah won the Nobel Prize for Literature in 2011.

        [C /(I)]   _Leymah won the Nobel Peace Prize in 2011._

    1. As a displaced person, Leymah lived in a crowded campground.

        [C / I] _____

    2. Leymah studied to help people suffering from trauma.

        [C / I] _____

    3. Leymah ran away from her husband and returned to her father's home.

        [C / I] _____

    4. Christian and Muslim women worked separately to build peace.

        [C / I] _____

5. Local and international media, soldiers, and politicians paid attention to the women.

[C / I] _____

6. Army leaders met for luxurious meals and peace talks at expensive conferences.

[C / I] _____

Listening

A Listen to the questions while scanning the passage and circle the best answers.

B
52-55

1. **a.** a victim   **b.** a college graduate   **c.** a female soldier   **d.** a TV reporter

2. **a.** abusive   **b.** gentle   **c.** hopeful   **d.** faithful

3. **a.** TV   **b.** Facebook   **c.** radio   **d.** Twitter

4. **a.** angry   **b.** relaxed   **c.** curious   **d.** sad

B Listen to the story and complete the script below.

B
56

Helping Refugees with the UN

Tomoko Ishihara worked with the UN to _____ displaced people in Syria. Her duties _____ arranging for the refugees to receive _____, bringing separated family members together, and _____ local government officials. Unexploded landmines are a _____

A girl sits next to UN-provided humanitarian aid packages at a refugee camp in Syria.

in many areas. When she learned the _____ of landmines, she arranged for _____ to remove them. She once _____ a young boy in an area with _____ landmines. Tomoko managed to safely _____ the boy to his parents. _____, she says, is one of her happiest _____ of working in Syria.

A discarded landmine on the ground in a village in Syria

Your Own Ideas

A Match the questions with the answers.

1. Have you ever tried to stop people from fighting? ____

2. Do you know where armies are fighting today? ____

3. Why do some people become violent? ____

4. What is the biggest cause of wars between countries? ____

5. What would you do if you were the leader of the world? ____

6. Do you think that your country could be involved in a war in the near future? ____

a. I would eliminate the borders between countries and unite the world.

b. Yes, I have. Two of my high school classmates were fighting, so I asked them to stop.

c. It could happen because our country has disagreements about islands with other countries. I hope not, though.

d. I think the shortage of natural resources is the biggest cause.

e. I don't know the names of the countries, but I think that people are fighting now in parts of the Middle East and Europe.

f. That is a hard question. Maybe they suffered trauma in childhood, or they think that other people will respect them for their power.

B Work in pairs. Take turns asking the questions above and answering with your own ideas.

Critical Thinking

A Read each statement below and write your opinion using one of the five key phrases in the example.

B 57

> **Ex.** Violence is wrong. We should solve all problems by talking.
>
> - **I strongly agree.** Honest discussions always lead to the best solutions.
> - **I somewhat agree.** As much as we can, we should solve problems without violence, but if someone attacks us, we don't have time for discussions.
> - **I'm not sure.** I can't decide. Maybe about half of our problems can be solved with honest conversations, but the other half requires violent action.
> - **I somewhat disagree.** We can't always converse with severely angry people. Sometimes police officers need to use violence to protect the peace.
> - **I strongly disagree.** The best way to stop a violent person is to use violence.

1. If more governments had women leaders, the world would be less violent.

   _____

2. The Japanese government should assist with peacebuilding in other countries.

   _____

3. Japan should not have a military of any type, including self-defense forces.

   _____

B Share your opinions with your classmates.

Taking Action

▶ Follow the steps to take action.

Step 1	In a small group, research peacebuilders not mentioned in this unit. Then, choose one to present on.
Step 2	Prepare to give a poster presentation about the person.
Step 3	Hang your posters in the classroom and take turns giving presentations.

Photo Credits:

クラス用音声CD有り（別売）

Positive Action
―People Making the World a Better Place

2023年3月1日　初版発行
2024年8月20日　第 2 刷

著　者　Greg Goodmacher
発行者　松村達生
発行所　センゲージ ラーニング株式会社
　　　　〒102-0073　東京都千代田区九段北1-11-11　第2フナトビル5階
　　　　電話 03-3511-4392　FAX 03-3511-4391
　　　　e-mail: eltjapan@cengage.com
　　　　copyright©2023 センゲージ ラーニング株式会社

装　丁　　足立友幸（parastyle inc.）
編集協力　飯尾緑子（parastyle inc.）
印刷・製本　株式会社エデュプレス

ISBN 978-4-86312-396-0